PERSONAL FINANCE

ESSENTIALS

Education
and Careers

VOLUME II

PERSONAL FINANCE

ESSENTIALS

Education
and Careers

VOLUME II

JANE S. LOPUS

An Infobase Learning Company

Personal Finance Essentials: Education and Careers
Copyright © 2012 Jane S. Lopus

Facts On File, Inc.
An imprint of Infobase Learning
132 West 31st Street
New York NY 10001

Library of Congress Cataloging-in-Publication Data
Heath, Julia A.
  Personal finance essentials / Julia A. Heath.
    v. cm.
  Vol. 2 by Jane S. Lopus.
  Includes bibliographical references and index.
  Contents: v. 1. Decision making and budgeting — v. 2. Education and careers — v. 3.
Credit and borrowing — v. 4. Saving and investing.
  ISBN 978-1-60413-986-0 (v. 1 : alk. paper) — ISBN 978-1-60413-987-7 (v. 2 : alk.
paper) — ISBN 978-1-60413-988-4 (v. 3 : alk. paper) — ISBN 978-1-60413-989-1 (v. 4
: alk. paper)
  1. Finance, Personal. I. Lopus, Jane S. II. Title.
  HG179.H374 2011
  332.024—dc22
                        2011004564

Facts On File books are available at special discounts when purchased in bulk quanti-
ties for businesses, associations, institutions, or sales promotions. Please call our Special
Sales Department in New York at (212) 967-8800 or (800) 322-8755.

You can find Facts On File on the World Wide Web at http://www.infobaselearning.com

Text design by Erik Lindstrom
Composition by Erik Lindstrom
Cover printed by Yurchak Printing, Landisville, Pa.
Book printed and bound by Yurchak Printing, Landisville, Pa.
Date printed: February 2012
Printed in the United States of America

Contents

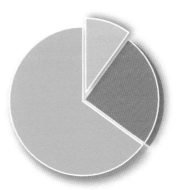

Introduction

What do you think of when you hear the term *financial literacy*? You probably have been hearing it a lot lately. As a result of the recent financial crisis, many people are calling for a greater level of financial literacy in the general population and among students in particular. But what does being "financially literate" mean? According to one popular notion, if someone knows how to write a check and balance his or her checkbook, then he or she is financially literate. Another view holds that someone who knows the benefits of saving is financially literate. These views all certainly reflect aspects of financial literacy, but they do not come close to describing what it really is.

In these volumes, we explore several topics: budgeting, getting an education, saving and investing, using credit wisely. Again, these are all components of what is commonly understood to be financial literacy. But also in these volumes is an emphasis on decision making—which is why it is the subject of the first volume in this series. The ability to make good decisions—identifying the important (and not-so-important) factors that should be considered, being able to weigh your options critically, being aware of the opportunity cost—is a skill that you will use over and over in your life. Being financially literate means that you understand how to make good decisions about money. So while the content of this set is an application of good decision-making skills, we hope that you recognize and apply the broader lessons to the non-financial aspects of your life as well.

When you hear the term *financial literacy*, do you feel excited to learn about it? Or anxious because you do not know anything about it, and you think it will be complicated? Or bored silly? Probably most people would choose the second or third answer—or maybe both. At the same time that there is general agreement that we need more financial literacy, it has gotten a bad rap. Financial literacy is often viewed as very complicated or, worse, extremely boring. It is neither. It just requires a change of perspective.

What if someone forced you to sit in a little box for several minutes each day—maybe for as long as an hour or more? You could not sleep, use your phone, or get up to walk around after a few minutes, you could not even let your mind wander. You would have to stay focused and just sit there. Does that seem like something you would be excited about doing? How excited were you when you learned to drive? When driving is described as it was above, it does not sound like something anyone would want to do. But you probably were very excited to learn to drive—not because of the physical movements associated with driving but because it represents independence and a rite of passage to adulthood. And it gets you from here to there.

The same is true with learning about financial literacy. Going through the mechanics of setting up a budget, a savings plan, investigating your education options, informing yourself so you do not fall victim to scams—none of that is very exciting in and of itself. But what it represents *is* exciting. It represents independence, being in control of your life. It represents a rite of passage—you are responsible for your financial future with the choices you make today. And it gets you from here to there. If you know or have talked to someone who does not have control over their financial lives, you have an idea of how consuming and debilitating the worry associated with that choice can be. The purpose of this set is to give you the skills you need to be purposeful in your decision making and to be able to take control of your life. Wherever your "here" is, with the help of these volumes, you can get to a better "there."

—Julia A. Heath and Jane S. Lopus

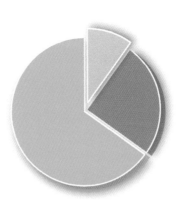

Education in the United States

Some of the most important decisions you will make in your life are decisions concerning your education. How long should you stay in school? What types of education are available to you, and which type is best for you? Once you decide on a career goal, how much and what type of education should you pursue to help you reach that goal? Your decisions about education will likely affect your future career, your income, and your lifestyle.

To make good decisions about your education, it helps to be familiar with the educational system in the United States. What types of education are available after high school? What is the difference between a trade school and a community college? How does a college differ from a university? What is a master's degree? This chapter provides an overview of how education in the United States is organized, with a focus on education after high school.

We discuss many of the terms related to postsecondary education. We also look at some issues involving the role of government in education: How do decisions taken by different levels of government affect education? How do public schools differ from private schools? How much education is compulsory? Let us explore these issues now.

LEVELS OF EDUCATION

Figure 1 is a diagram of the different levels of education, types of schools, and types of degrees generally available in the United States. The main levels of education available are elementary or primary education, secondary education, and postsecondary or higher education. Postsecondary education can be divided into undergraduate and postgraduate levels.

Elementary and Secondary (K-12) Education

In the United States, education from kindergarten through high school (12th grade) is often called *K-12 education. Elementary education* is also called primary education. Elementary schools usually include grades one through six and serve students aged six through 11. As shown in the preceding diagram, there are several different structures for the level of education between elementary schools and high schools. Some school districts have *middle schools* or junior high schools for students aged 11 through 13 or 14. Other school districts offer combined junior and senior high schools beginning in seventh grade. And in some districts students attend elementary schools through eighth grade and then advance straight to high schools.

U.S. *high schools,* sometimes called senior high schools, frequently include grades nine or 10 through 12 and serve students between the ages of 14 and 18. High

Fig 1.1 The Structure of Education in the United States

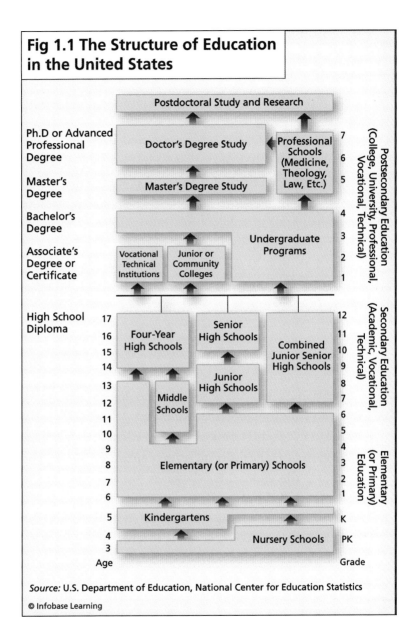

Source: U.S. Department of Education, National Center for Education Statistics

© Infobase Learning

schools often offer a wide range of courses in both academic and vocational areas in order to serve the needs of both college-bound students and students who will join the workforce soon after high school. Upon meeting school requirements, you graduate from high school with a high school diploma. This diploma is a certificate indicating that you have completed the necessary coursework and earned overall passing grades in high school courses.

Graduating from high school and earning a high school diploma is a major accomplishment. However, for most U.S. students, high school graduation is a step toward acquiring more advanced education. Most U.S. students enroll in colleges or universities very soon after completing high school. According to the Bureau of Labor Statistics, 70 percent of those who graduated from high school in 2009 were enrolled in colleges or universities in October 2009.

Postsecondary Education: Undergraduate Level

Postsecondary education, also called higher education, refers to education obtained after high school. This is referred to in general terms as a *college education.* A college education can take different forms depending on the type of school you choose. As shown in the diagram, at the *undergraduate* level (before receiving a college degree) the types of institutions you may attend can be divided into the categories of vocational or technical institutions, junior or community colleges, and four-year colleges or universities.

Vocational or technical institutions are sometimes also called career or trade schools. These institutions may have names that designate themselves as schools, colleges, or (less frequently) universities. They are designed to teach you a specific job or trade. General business schools, which may focus on keyboarding, bookkeeping, and computer literacy, also fall into this category. You may find vocational colleges that offer a wide variety of programs such as electronics, cosmetology, vocational nursing, medical billing, personal fitness assistance, criminal justice, and legal assistance. Some vocational colleges specialize in certain areas such as health careers, beauty careers, or office assistance careers. Their programs frequently last two years or less. Those who complete a program may receive a diploma or certificate depending on the type of program and the institution where they enroll. These schools may be public or private and the cost of attending varies widely. To be admitted to a vocational or technical institution, you typically need a high school diploma. For many institutions this is the only requirement for admission.

Community colleges, sometimes called junior colleges, offer two-year programs leading to associate degrees. A high school diploma is generally required for admission, although high school students can sometimes take courses at local community colleges before they graduate from high schools. The term community college is more common today than junior college, reflecting the idea that the colleges usually serve students from the local community.

Programs in community colleges follow two main strands. Many students who earn Associate of Arts or Associate of Science degrees plan to transfer to four-year colleges or universities, and the coursework completed is roughly equivalent to completing the first two years at four-year colleges and universities. Community colleges may have articulation agreements with four-year institutions that help students transfer credits earned toward a four-year college degree. However, community colleges also offer programs leading to certification for specific

A group of college graduates. According to the National Center for Education Statistics, about 42 percent of those awarded a college degree eventually enroll in postgraduate education. *(Shutterstock)*

careers such as nursing, accounting, or early childhood education. In this way, their programs may compete with vocational colleges. Community colleges are usually tax-supported public institutions and are often one of the least costly ways of obtaining a two-year college education.

In most cases, when someone is a college graduate or receives a college degree, this means that he or she has received a bachelor's degree from a *four-year college* or *university.* These institutions offer a variety of *majors* (areas of specialization) and regularly require students to complete a wide variety of courses to receive a broad, general education in addition to courses in their major field. Four-year colleges and universities may be public or private, small or large. Their quality is assessed through independent organizations that are not affiliated with the U.S. government. Admission requirements vary greatly, and earning certain scores on entrance exams such as the Scholastic Aptitude Test (SAT) or American College Testing examination (ACT) are frequently required for admission.

Although the terms college and university are often used interchangeably, colleges often limit their offerings to four-year undergraduate degrees whereas universities also offer more advanced degrees. Universities are usually larger than colleges and may be organized to contain different colleges such as a college of business and a college of arts and sciences.

Many factors go into the decision of choosing the right college. The costs and benefits of education, choosing the right level of education and the right college for you, and how your education relates to your career will be discussed in later chapters. We will also discuss the college admissions process.

Postsecondary education: Postgraduate Level

About 42 percent of those receiving a college degree eventually enroll in *postgraduate education* (http://nces. ed.gov.) Postgraduate education means education received after graduating from a four-year college or university. Our diagram shows four different types of postgraduate studies: master's degrees, doctorate degrees, professional degrees, and postdoctoral study. Another type of postgraduate study, not shown on the diagram, is postgraduate study at a college or university leading to a professional certificate or license, but not to a specific degree. For example, in some states teachers study to earn teaching certificates or licenses after completing college.

Master's degrees are a type of postsecondary education usually involving two years of advanced study in a specific field such as business or education. A common master's degree is an MBA, or Masters of Business Administration. A *Ph.D.*, or doctorate, involves three to five years of graduate study and writing a dissertation involving original research in the chosen field. Ph.D. stands for doctor of philosophy, although Ph.D.'s are earned in many fields and not just in philosophy. A Ph.D. may follow a master's degree but this is often not required. Those who earn Ph.D.'s may be called a "doctor" in their field (a doctor of economics, for example) although they are not medical doctors. Certain jobs require Ph.D.'s, such as university professors and some research positions. Soon after completing a Ph.D., some students engage in *post-doctoral study* or research to further focus on their area of study. These programs are often funded by a university or other research institution.

Some professions require you to graduate from a *professional school* and pass specialized exams after you earn your undergraduate degree. For example, in order to be a medical doctor, a dentist, or a lawyer, you must graduate from a medical school, a dental school, or a law school and pass examinations to practice your profession. These professional schools are usually part of universities. Doctors attend medical school for four years, followed by three to seven years in a residency where they practice their specialization. Dental school lasts four years, but more years are required for specialized areas such as orthodontics. Law schools are most often three years. Chapter 5 provides more information on the level and type of education necessary for different careers.

THE ROLE OF GOVERNMENT

All levels of government in the United States—federal, state, and local—play important roles in administering educational programs from pre-kindergarten through postdoctoral levels. However education is much more *decentralized* in the United States than in many other countries. This means that most decisions are made at the local level rather than at the national level. At the core of the issue of the role of government in education is the distinction between public schools and private schools.

Public Schools versus Private Schools

Public schools and colleges are those that are operated by state and local governments. In fact, one definition of the word public is "maintained at the public expense and under public control." Examples of public institutions are public libraries, public roads, and public schools. The right to a free public education in the United States is guaranteed by the constitutions of all 50 states. Although K-12 education is technically free in all 50 states, parents are sometimes asked to contribute to pay for supplies, books, and sports fees for their students.

Private schools and colleges are not formally affiliated with a government organization. Private schools are common in the United States from the pre-kindergarten level through the graduate and professional school levels. Most students pay tuition and other fees to attend private schools. The amount of these fees varies depending on the type of private school. At the K-12 level, fees at local religious schools may be relatively low whereas tuition and fees at some private boarding schools may be as high as those at prestigious private colleges and universities.

Private schools and colleges may be *nonprofit* institutions, meaning that they use any profits earned to achieve the goals of the school rather than distributing profits to owners or shareholders. Or private schools and colleges may be *for-profit* businesses, meaning that any profits earned may be distributed to owners or shareholders. Many career, trade, or technical schools are for-profit businesses. For-profit schools at the K-12 levels are less common than at the pre-kindergarten and postsecondary levels.

Private schools accounted for between 10 and 11 percent of pre-kindergarten through 12th grade enrollment in the United States in 2007. The remaining 89–90 percent of students were enrolled in public schools (www. NCES.ed.gov.) There are many different types of K-12 private schools including charter schools, boarding schools, religiously-affiliated schools, military schools, schools focusing on the arts or other specific fields, and schools restricting enrollment to male or female students.

At the postsecondary level, about 73 percent of all students enrolled were in public institutions in 2006. Nineteen percent were enrolled in private nonprofit institutions and 8 percent in private for-profit institutions. These figures include enrollment in two-year, four-year, graduate, and professional institutions. Breaking down the numbers by level of education, we find that enrollment in public institutions accounted for about 94 percent of those enrolled in two-year colleges, 65 percent of those in four-year colleges, 53 percent of those in graduate schools, and 40 percent of those in professional schools (www.NCES.ed.gov.)

Since public education is available in the United States and is free at the K-12 level, why do some families choose private education, which can cost substantially more? In some cases, families believe that the quality of a private education is superior to that of the available public education and is therefore worth the extra cost. In other cases, the private schools may offer different courses or services than public schools, such as religious instruction or after-school day care. Similar factors affect decisions to attend private postsecondary institutions when less expensive public institutions may be available. Some private post-secondary institutions may be perceived to be of higher quality or may offer potentially desirable options such as smaller classes. Weighing the costs and benefits of different types of postsecondary education will be explored more thoroughly in chapter 4.

Compulsory Education

One role for government to play in education is to decide how much education is required. *Compulsory education* means education that is required by law. In the United States, laws mandating how much education is compulsory are set by individual states. All 50 states require children to be enrolled in public or private school or to be home-schooled for a certain number of years or grades. Requirements for the age for starting school vary between ages five and eight, with 32 states requiring students to begin their education by age six. All states require education into high school, with 26 states mandating that students stay in school through age 16. The other states mandate that students stay in school through age 17 or 18. Some states require students to stay in school through a certain grade rather than a specified age. Most states grant exceptions to their compulsory polices in cases where students have completed coursework early or have enrolled in another type of education program (www.

All states require education to high school, with 26 states mandating that students stay in school through age 16. *(Shutterstock)*

ncsl.org.) Postsecondary education is not compulsory in the United States.

The Role of the Federal Government

The federal government plays a limited role in establishing educational policies in the United States. In fact, the role of the federal government is limited by the Tenth Amendment of the U.S. Constitution, which says "The powers not delegated to the United States by the Constitution, nor prohibited by it to the States, are reserved to the States respectively, or to the people." This means that since the constitution does not expressly give the federal government control over education, this power goes to the states or to individuals.

Because the role of the federal government is limited in education does not mean that the federal government has no influence or interest in education. In fact, the federal government leads many educational reform programs, administers programs approved by congress, enforces civil rights laws that deal with education, and provides research about education. It does not, however, own or control universities (except for military academies), license or accredit schools or universities, control curricula, or determine budgets for local school districts (www2.ed.gov.).

The federal government does provide funding for education. Figure 1.2 shows the distribution of total spending on K-12 education in the United States by federal, state, and local governments. Although the federal government's share of education spending is small compared to spending by state and local governments, the percentage share is growing. In 1990–91, the federal government's share was less than 6 percent. As of 2005, about 8 percent of spending on K-12 education came from the federal government (www2.ed.gov.). The following graph also indicates that overall spending on public education has increased dramatically over this period.

The Role of State Governments

The governments of the 50 U.S. states have direct control over most aspects of education at the elementary, secondary, and postsecondary levels. Education is the largest item in the budgets of all 50 states. Each state has its own constitution that determines how the state controls education. However, state laws must be consistent with federally guaranteed constitutional rights. Common functions for states with respect to education include providing funding for public education at all levels, establishing

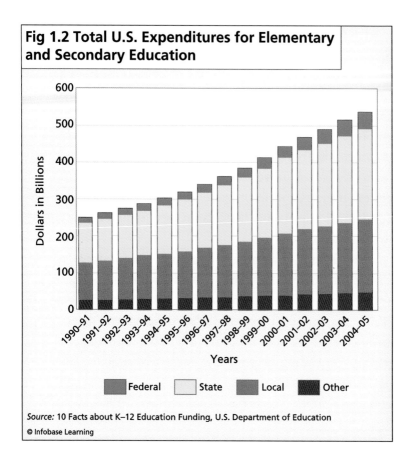

Fig 1.2 Total U.S. Expenditures for Elementary and Secondary Education

Dollars in Billions

Years

Federal State Local Other

Source: 10 Facts about K–12 Education Funding, U.S. Department of Education

© Infobase Learning

policies for curricula, textbooks, standards, and testing, licensing private schools, overseeing the administration of state colleges and universities, and setting standards for teachers.

The Role of Local Governments

A strong degree of local control over education is the core of the organization of the U.S. educational system. There are more than 14,000 local school districts in the United States that are in charge of the day-to-day operations of schools, including hiring and supervising teachers. School districts raise money for schools, usually through property taxes. Locally-elected Boards of Education govern school districts and often hold open meetings to inform members of the community about policies and procedures affecting the local schools. School Board elections are open to all of the voting public in the local school district, demonstrating the idea that local schools are important to all of the community and not just to those who attend or have children in the schools. School district budgets are separate from other local budgets such as those of cities and counties.

In addition to local governments, other members of local communities also influence school district decisions. This includes parents and parent organizations that are active in local schools and school-community partnerships, such as cooperative agreements between local businesses and schools.

SUMMARY

The U.S. educational system is highly decentralized with most decisions about education administration made at the state or local levels. The main levels of education available in the United States are elementary, secondary, and postsecondary. Education is generally compulsory from age six through age 16, 17, or 18. Most students attend public schools at both the K-12 and postsecondary levels of education. The major types of institutions offering undergraduate postsecondary education are vocational institutions, community colleges, and four-year colleges and universities. Having knowledge about the different levels of education available after high school and the different types of postsecondary schools can be helpful in making important decisions about how long to stay in school, which type of postsecondary institution to attend, and which college is best for you.

2

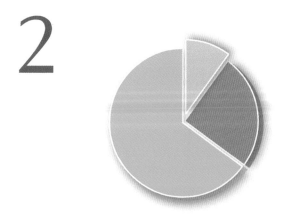

The Costs of a College Education and How to Pay for It

Deciding whether to go to college or not is one of the most important decisions you will make in your life. What things should you consider when making that decision? Going to college can provide many benefits to you and to others, which will be discussed in chapter 3. But obtaining a higher education can also be costly. What are some of the costs involved in going to college? How do economists view costs? How do costs differ depending on the type of college that you choose? How can you get enough money to finance your education? These are some of the questions that will be answered in this chapter.

Opportunity Costs of a College Education

When you think about the cost of getting an education, you probably think in terms of the actual dollars you will need to spend. You will need to find a way to pay for out-of-pocket expenses like tuition and fees, books, transportation, and so on. And these monetary costs are important. But economists view costs in a different way. Economists look at opportunity costs. *Opportunity cost* is what you give up when you have to make a choice. Let us investigate the opportunity cost idea in more detail and see how it applies to education.

Whenever you have to make a choice, you have to give something up. For example, suppose your friend offers to give you either an apple or an orange. If you choose the apple, you give up being able to have the orange. Because you had to choose between the apple and the orange, there was a cost involved—in this case, the orange. Economists call this opportunity cost. The opportunity cost of choosing the apple is the orange that you gave up because you chose the apple. Note that you did not have to pay any money. But there was still an opportunity cost to you because you had to make a choice. If you had chosen the orange, the opportunity cost would have been the apple.

Now let us look at the opportunity costs involved with deciding to continue your education and to go to college for four years. Ask yourself what you would be doing if you did not go to college. Would you be working in a full-time job? Would you get married and start a family? Would you join the military? What would be the next best alternative use of your time over the next four years? That would be the opportunity cost of your deciding to go to college.

Assume that if you did not go to college, you would be working in a full-time job as a receptionist for a real estate firm. You would earn $12 an hour, plus benefits including a contribution toward medical insurance. You would be getting training and work experience. At the

According to the Bureau of Labor Statistics, 70 percent of recent high school graduates not enrolled in college in fall 2009 partici-pated in the labor force. *(Shutterstock)*

end of four years, you may be ready to move up into a job with more responsibilities and higher pay. What would be your opportunity costs of going to college? Your opportunity costs would include the income, benefits, training, and experience that you could be earning if you chose to work instead of going to college.

When economists analyze opportunity costs of something like going to college, they consider both the actual money paid as well as the opportunity costs that do not involve the payment of money. This is part of the economic way of thinking. Thinking about opportunity costs can help you to make good choices by comparing the value of the alternatives available to you.

Monetary Costs of a College Education

How much it costs in dollars to get a college degree varies widely and depends on many factors. How much you pay will depend on whether you attend a two-year college or a four-year college or university and whether you attend a private school or a public school. How much you pay will also depend on the type and amount of financial aid—grants, scholarships, and loans—for which you qualify. Tuition and fees are a major expense category. Your room and board expenses will depend on whether you live at home or live at the college. Transportation costs too many need to be taken into consideration. You also need to consider the cost of books and supplies such as notebooks, pens, and a computer. Costs of books and supplies can vary depending on what you choose to study. There are also miscellaneous personal expenses such as laundry and your phone bill. The following list summarizes both opportunity costs and monetary costs of going to college.

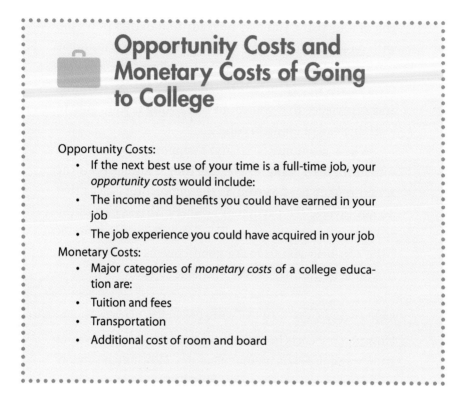

Opportunity Costs and Monetary Costs of Going to College

Opportunity Costs:
- If the next best use of your time is a full-time job, your *opportunity costs* would include:
- The income and benefits you could have earned in your job
- The job experience you could have acquired in your job

Monetary Costs:
- Major categories of *monetary costs* of a college education are:
- Tuition and fees
- Transportation
- Additional cost of room and board

It is important to understand that the college expenses you should consider are the additional expenses that you would incur because you go college, and not expenses you would also incur if you did not go to college. For example, if your food would cost you $200 if you did not go to college but $250 if you do go to college, it is the additional $50 that is the important college cost. You would be paying $200 regardless of what you did. If your miscellaneous expenses such as doing your laundry and paying your phone bill would be $100 a month if you went to college and $100 a month if you did not go to college, then there are no additional costs for going to college. Economists use the terms *marginal costs* or incremental costs when they look at how much costs change as a result of doing something, in this case going to college. It is the marginal or incremental costs that tell you the additional costs you pay to go to college versus doing something else.

Tuition and Fees

For most students, tuition and fees are the major college cost. According to the College Board (www.collegeboard. com), the average cost of tuition and fees at two-year colleges was $2,544 in 2009. At four-year public colleges, the average cost of tuition and fees was $7,020 for students who attend a school in their state. However, if you attend a public four-year college in a state where you are not a resident, you can expect to pay an extra $11,528 in tuition and fees on average. The average cost of tuition and fees in private four-year colleges was $26,273 in 2009. These figures are shown in the following table. Keep in mind that these are averages. The college where you apply may have either lower or higher costs.

Community colleges are generally less expensive than other colleges because of government subsidies that keep costs down for the students. The philosophy behind community colleges is to have low-cost higher education available for almost everyone. Public universities

AVERAGE TUITION AND FEES FOR DIFFERENT TYPES OF COLLEGES (2009)

TYPE OF COLLEGE	AVERAGE TUITION AND FEES
Public two-year colleges	$2,544

Public four-year colleges
    in-state students
    out-of-state students
	$7,020
	$18,548

Private four-year colleges	$26,273

Source: What It Costs to Go to College: www.collegeboard.com

COSTS OF TUITION, FEES, AND ROOM AND BOARD AT FOUR FOUR-YEAR COLLEGES (2010)

PUBLIC	TUITION	FEES	ROOM AND BOARD
University of Michigan Ann Arbor, MI	In state: $12,400 Out state: $36,163	$189	$8,924
Boise State University Boise, ID	In state: $3,106 Out state: $12,110	$1,758	$5,602
PRIVATE	TUITION	FEES	ROOM AND BOARD
Harvard University Cambridge, MA	$33,696	$3,316	$11,856
York College of PA York, PA	$13,000	$1,460	$8,080

Source: What will college run you? 2010. CNNMoney.com

usually have lower tuition and fees than private universities, again due to government support for the public universities. Attending a public university in your state is usually cheaper than attending a public university in another state. This is because residents of a state pay more taxes to support the public universities within the state, so it is thought to be fair that students who live in the state should be charged less than those whose families do not pay the state taxes.

The table above shows the cost of tuition, fees, and room and board for four different four-year colleges and universities. The schools listed in the table are not necessarily the highest cost or lowest cost colleges in the public and private categories, but were chosen to show the variations of the costs among these types of institutions. The University of Michigan, Ann Arbor and Boise State University are both state-supported public institutions. Tuition for an in-state student attending the University of Michigan was $12,400 in 2010, whereas in-state tuition at Boise State was $3,106. Out-of-state tuition at the University of Michigan was $36,163 and $12,110 at Boise State. Harvard University and York College of Pennsylvania are both private four-year colleges, but Harvard tuition was $33,696 in 2010 while tuition at York College of Pennsylvania was $13,000. When investigating the costs of different schools, it is important to look at the costs of the individual schools and not just the averages for the type of school you are considering.

What Do You Really Pay?

Many students end up paying much less that what a college's advertised tuition, fees, and other expenses indicate that it would cost. This is because many types of financial aid are available. According to CBSMoneyWatch.com, most parents do not understand that the official "sticker prices" of attending college are meaningless because many colleges and universities regularly offer significant discounts to qualified students.

To end this confusion, the U.S. government is requiring colleges and universities to install "net price calculators" on their Web sites by fall 2011. The intent of the Web site calculators is to help prospective college students and their parents figure out the net price, or the actual dollar cost, of attending a college after taking into account the grants, scholarships, and other aid for which a student may qualify. To use the calculators, you answer questions on the college Web site that help the college determine the type of financial assistance you may receive. Then you receive an estimate that shows how much the college may really cost if you received that much assistance. While the calculators may be helpful, keep in mind that they only provide estimates. The final amount that you really pay will be determined with the financial aid office once you apply to the college and may also depend on other aid that you may receive.

FINANCING A COLLEGE EDUCATION

Since many students end up paying far less than the official cost of tuition and other expenses, you should not count out a school just because it appears to be too expensive. You should thoroughly investigate the financial options available to you to help you pay for college. There are many different types of financial aid available to help you pay for college, and there are different sources of financial aid. We will first look at the types of financial aid that are available.[1]

Types of Financial Aid: Need-based and Non-need-based

One way to look at the different types of financial aid is to look at need-based financial aid and non–need-based financial aid. *Need-based financial aid* is for students who do not have enough money to pay for their own college education. Depending on the student's age and other

TYPES OF FINANCIAL AID

Need-based and non-need-based
Scholarships
Grants
Loans
Work programs
Aid based on:
   Major field of study
   Athletics
   Military
   Student characteristics

[1]Information in this section is in part based on materials provided by the National Association of Student Financial Aid Administrators, www.nasfaa.org.

factors, the income and assets of the student's family are often also taken into consideration. To qualify for need-based financial aid, you and your family fill out applications documenting that you do not have enough money and other financial assets to pay for the education yourself.

Students who do not qualify for need-based financial aid may qualify for aid based on merit, such as having very high scores on college entrance exams or being a superior athlete. This is called *non–need-based financial aid* or *merit-based financial aid*. Merit-based financial aid is given for factors other than financial need. There are many different areas for non–need-based financial aid in addition to high test scores and athletic ability. These include high school grades, service to the community, talent such as singing or dancing, and leadership. Financial aid based on ethnicity and religious background may also be non–need-based.

Types of Financial Aid: Scholarships, Grants, Loans, and Work

You may receive either need-based or merit-based financial aid in a number of ways. We can divide types of financial aid into categories of scholarships, grants, loans, and work programs. A *scholarship* is a type of financial aid to further education that does not have to be repaid. Scholarships are often merit-based and awarded on the basis of academic or athletic talent, interest in studying certain subjects, or being part of a certain minority group. Many scholarships are awarded on the basis of a combination of merit and need. Scholarships are given by a variety or organizations including colleges themselves, businesses, and community organizations. Scholarships are often given to promote the goals of the person or

According to the National Center for Education Statistics, 79.5 percent of full-time undergraduates received some form of financial aid in 2007–08. *(Shutterstock)*

organization contributing to the scholarship. For example, the American Society of Composers, Authors, and Publishers offers a number of scholarships that can help talented music students pay for college. To keep a scholarship, students frequently must fulfill certain requirements such as maintaining a certain grade point average while in college.

As with a scholarship, a grant does not have to be repaid. *Grants* are a type of financial aid most often offered by the federal or state governments. Grants are usually need-based and are usually not tied to special talents or achievements. The federal government offers the largest amount of grant money for college in the United States.

Private nonprofit organizations sometimes offer grants for college education also. At the graduate level, students who receive grants are often required to complete a project involving a certain type of research. Grants are also available for things other than college such as starting a business. *Fellowships* are like grants and are financial aid offered by a university or other organization, usually for graduate study.

Another common way to get money for college is to borrow it. *Student loans* are money that you borrow for college and that you must pay back. You usually do not need to begin paying back a student loan until after you have graduated from college. Generally when you borrow money, you are expected to pay back the amount that you borrowed plus interest. *Interest* is the cost you pay for borrowing money. The *interest rate* on the loan is the percentage of the total amount borrowed that you must pay back in interest.

How much you are required to pay back for a student loan often depends on how much need you are determined to have. Sometimes need-based loans do not require students to repay the interest. Sometimes non–need-based loans require repayment of the interest that accrued while you were in school as well as the interest that accrues when you are out of school. Student loans often charge lower interest than other types of loans because the government subsidizes the interest payments on the loans. Student loans are available for the parents of college students as well as to the students themselves.

There are some types of student loans that do not have to be repaid under certain circumstances. For example, the government may have a program to loan money to students studying to become a nurse. If the student completes the education and works as a nurse for a certain period of time, the loan may be "forgiven." This means that the nurse would not have to repay the loan. The purpose of loan programs like this is to encourage students to enter professions where there is a perceived need.

Many colleges have programs where they give you a job or help you find a job so you can earn money to help you pay for your educational expenses. These programs are called *work-study programs.* Participating in work-study programs is frequently need-based. Some work-study jobs may be related to your interests and your field of study. For example, a biology major may be offered a job working in a biology lab on campus. In other cases, the job you are offered may involve working in a campus cafeteria or dormitory and the job may not be related to your interests or what you are studying. Other work-study jobs may be with businesses off campus. Holding a job while attending college can give you valuable work experience. If you have a work-study job, it is important to learn to allocate your time so that you are able to perform well both in your academic classes as well as on the job.

Types of Financial Aid: Based on Major, Athletics, Military, and Student Characteristics

Another way to look at types of financial aid available is to focus specifically on financial aid available to students majoring in different fields, for athletes, for military academies, and for students with different characteristics. These types of financial aid may be need-based or non–need-based or a combination of the two.

College students specialize in a field of study called their *major.* Your major represents your primary academic interest and the area where you have taken the most courses. Sometimes scholarships and grants are available to students who major in a certain subject or area such as engineering or performing arts. These awards may be offered through a college, by the government, or through another organization. For example, in 2010 the California School Library Association offered a $1,500 scholarship to a student living in Southern California who is studying to become a school librarian. Iowa State University offered a $200 scholarship to an incoming freshman majoring in agricultural business or economics. The federal government offered grants up to $4,000 per year to those who intend to teach in elementary or secondary schools that serve students from low-income families.

Athletic scholarships are most often offered through sports programs at individual colleges and universities. Sometimes talented athletes are recruited by a sports program at a particular college and offered a scholarship in return for a promise to play on a team. In other cases, student athletes contact the coaches of their sport at colleges they may be interested in attending to determine the availability of athletic scholarships. Although a few large universities are often featured on television for sports such as football and basketball, athletic scholarships are available at many smaller schools and in other sports also.

Students attending military academies such as the United States Military Academy at West Point receive full scholarships and have other expenses of their education covered. After graduating, students agree to serve in the armed forces for an agreed-upon number of years. West point graduates serve as officers in the U.S. Army for five years after graduation. The U.S. Navy, Air Force, Coast Guard, and Merchant Marines also have academies where students who are accepted earn college degrees and are awarded full scholarships.

U.S. Army cadets recite a pledge during their commencement ceremony at the U.S. Military Academy at West Point, N.Y. West Point graduates must serve as officers in the U.S. Army for five years. *(Defense Imagery)*

There are other scholarships available to students who have certain characteristics. For example, students who are dependents of military veterans may receive scholarships offered by organizations such as the Air Force Aid Society and the Fleet Reserve Association. Several organizations offer scholarships to gay, lesbian, bisexual, and transgender students. Students who are members of racial minority groups may apply for scholarships from organizations such as the United Negro College Fund or the American Indian College Fund. There are scholarships available specifically for women offered through social sororities and other organizations. There are scholarships for students with disabilities offered by organizations such as the Alexander Graham Bell Association for the Deaf and Hard of Hearing and the American Council for the Blind.

SOURCES OF FINANCIAL AID AND FINANCIAL AID INFORMATION

Finding out about all of the scholarships, grants, loans, and work programs available to help you pay for college may sound like a big task, and it is. However there are steps you can take to help you locate and sort through the information available. One thing you should consider is that good information about reputable financial aid programs is available for free. Although there are organizations who promise to help you locate scholarships for a fee, make sure that what they are offering is worth the price they charge you.

Federal Financial Aid

The federal government is the largest source of financial aid for college students. Information about the different types of federal financial aid is available at http://studentaid.ed.gov. Federal financial aid programs for

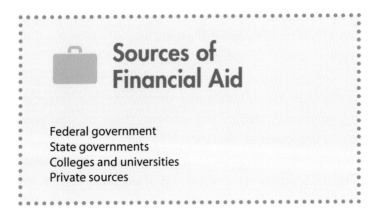

Sources of Financial Aid

Federal government
State governments
Colleges and universities
Private sources

undergraduate students are divided into the categories of grants, campus-based aid, Stafford Loans, and PLUS Loans (Parent Loans.) The amount and types of aid available changes over time, so you need to check the government's Web site to see what is available when you are ready to apply. For example, beginning with the 2010–11 award year, the Iraq and Afghanistan Service Grant was available for students whose parent or guardian was in the U.S. Armed Forces and died as a result of service performed in Iraq or Afghanistan.

You may apply for all types of federal student financial aid with one form, the FAFSA. *FAFSA* stands for Free Application for Federal Student Aid. The form is available at www.fafsa.ed.gov. The Web site contains detailed instructions for filling out the form and information about the different types of federal student aid programs. If your parents apply for a PLUS Loan to help pay for your education, they will fill out a different application form.

The *Federal Pell Grant* is a need-based grant that does not need to be repaid. In 2010–11, Pell grants offered students up to $5,550 per year. The amount awarded depends on the student's need, the costs of attending school, and part-time or full-time student status. To qualify, you must be enrolled at least half-time in a program leading to an associate or bachelor's degree or certificate. Students receiving Federal Pell grants may also receive other types of federal financial aid.

Campus-based aid programs consist of three programs that are administered directly by the financial aid offices of participating schools. These are the Federal Supplemental Educational Opportunity Grants (FSEOG), Federal Work-Study (FWS), and Federal Perkins Loan programs. The amount of aid you receive from these programs depends on your financial need as well as how much money is available at your school. FSEOG grants are provided to students with the greatest financial need. FWS provides part-time jobs for students with financial need, and you are paid directly by your school for work. Federal Perkins Loans are low-interest loans for students with great financial need. Your school serves as the lender, although the loan is from government funds. You begin to repay the loan nine months after you graduate or leave school.

Like Perkins loans, *Stafford Loans* are low-interest loans for students with financial need to help finance education at a four-year college, community college, or trade school. Students receiving Stafford loans borrow from the U.S. Department of Education through their school. Stafford Loans do not require as much financial need as Perkins loans. You begin paying back a Stafford Loan six months after graduating or leaving school.

Direct PLUS Loans for Parents are loans that a parent can apply for to pay for a dependent child's education. The parent must have good credit and is responsible for paying off the loan. Parents may borrow up to the cost of attending the college less any other financial aid received by the student. The interest rate is higher on PLUS loans than on Perkins and Stafford Loans. The parent must begin repaying the loan 60 days after the final disbursement was made to the student.

State Financial Aid

State governments also provide financial aid to students to help pay for higher education. The type, amount, qualifications, and applications for financial aid vary from state to state, so you need to investigate what is available in the state where you live. If you plan to attend college in a state other than where you live, you should also investigate what financial aid is available in that state. You should contact state governments to find the agency that is in charge of financial aid for college in the states that pertain to you.

In many cases, to qualify for state financial aid for education you need to be a resident of the state and attending college in the state where you are applying. To be a legal resident of a state, you must have lived in the state for a certain number of consecutive months, for example for 12 months. Contacting the state agency that is in charge of higher education in your state is a good place to find out about what aid may be available for you. Your college financial aid office and high school college and career center may also be good sources of information.

Financial Aid from Your College

Most colleges will have financial aid available for some of their students. Depending on the school, the aid available may include both need-based and non–need-based grants and scholarships, as well as loans and work-study programs. Finding out what financial aid is available to you at the colleges you are considering may be very valuable in helping you decide where to attend college. Some expensive and prestigious schools advertise that they will provide financial aid for all educational expenses for all students with financial need who are admitted. College Web sites, college financial aid workers, and high school college counselors should be able to provide you with helpful information about financial aid available from different colleges.

Private Sources of Financial Aid

There are many private businesses and other organizations that offer scholarships for college. Some of these organizations are locally based and may offer scholarships to students who live in the local community. Sometimes the company where a parent works offers scholarships to students of workers. It may be worthwhile to contact your local government to see if they have grants or scholarships for local students. Your local chamber of commerce may know if local businesses provide scholarships. Also, private financial institutions such as banks frequently offer student loans at competitive interest rates.

Many large corporations such as Target, Walmart, Apple, McDonald's, and Disney offer scholarships. For example, in 2010, Coca-Cola provided $5,000 to an American Indian student who would be the first in the family to attend college at a tribal college or university. Best Buy offered $1,000 scholarships to students involved in community service or work experience. There are several free and independent Web sites that offer information about scholarships available from private sources, including www.Scholarships.com and www.CollegeScholarships.org. However, you should always cross check information from Web sites with information provided by the companies and organizations themselves.

SUMMARY

Thinking about how much it costs to earn a college degree and how you will get the money you need is a serious undertaking. It involves assessing the opportunity costs that exist in addition to the monetary costs and comparing the costs of different types of institutions. It involves learning about different types of financial aid and where to obtain information on the different types of aid available. These are some of the issues that have been addressed in this chapter. For many students, the cost of education affects the decision about where to go to college. Being informed about what your education will cost and the options available for financial aid are good steps in making the decision about your future education. The other part of the picture is the benefits of education, which is the topic of the next chapter.

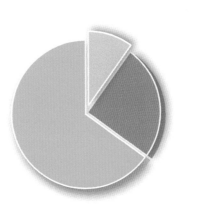

3

The Benefits
of Education

You are probably planning to get a good job when you finish school. Your skills and abilities as a worker, and your income, will depend in part on your formal education as well as on your training on-the-job. An important decision you have to make is how much formal education you should get to qualify for a good job. Continuing your education has other benefits in addition to increased income. What are the advantages of finishing high school? What are the advantages of getting as associate's degree or a bachelor's degree? Should you plan to get an advanced degree?

When you stay in school and continue your education, you are *investing in human capital*. Human capital refers to a person's knowledge and skills. Investing in human capital makes you a better worker. It is an investment because education and training increase your knowledge and your abilities, much like investing in a factory increases the output of a business. In both cases, investment means that someone is devoting resources and time to achieve or produce something in the future. In the case of human capital, you are devoting your resources and time to increase what you know and your ability to accomplish things. This will enable you to perform better in your job and earn a higher income, among other benefits. You also acquire human capital from on-the-job training. *On-the-job training* refers to the training and skills a worker learns while at work. On-the-job training can be specific to a job or it can be more general, where skills can transfer to other jobs. However, much education is acquired in school before you enter the workforce.

Continuing your education and investing in human capital provides many benefits both to you and to others. You probably think mostly about the benefits that accrue to you personally, such as higher expected income and the pleasure you get from learning. But there are *external benefits* also. External benefits of education are the benefits that help others in society in addition to you and the provider of your education. Society benefits from having a more educated population in many ways. For example, people who learn to read can obey signs and traffic signals, which helps to prevent accidents. External benefits to education provide a rationale for why the government provides subsidies for many types of education.

Making a decision about whether or not to continue your education involves much the same decision-making process as making other decisions. You need to figure out the costs and benefits of continuing your education. In chapter 2, we looked at the costs of education, both the out-of-pocket costs and the opportunity costs. In this chapter, we will look at the evidence about the benefits of education. We will investigate both personal benefits and external benefits. If you decide that your personal benefits of continuing your education are greater than the costs, then you should decide to continue your education.

PERSONAL BENEFITS OF EDUCATION
Education, Weekly Earnings, and Unemployment

One very important personal benefit of education is that more education frequently results in higher incomes. There are many reasons why your income may be different from that of other people, including your occupation, whether you work full-time or part-time, the supply and demand for workers in your field, the supply and demand for the goods and services you produce, and how good you are at your job. However, in general the more education you have, the more likely it is that you will earn a higher income. And the more education you have, the less likely it is that you will become unemployed.

Table 3.1 shows the relationship between the unemployment rate, the level of education, and median weekly earnings for full-time workers age 25 and over in 2009. *Median* earnings means that half of the people in the category earned above that level of weekly income, and half of the people in that category earned below that level of weekly income. The table shows that those who did not finish high school had a median income of $454 per week. Finishing high school raised the median income to $626 per week, and attending some college raised it another $73 per week, to $699. Those who earned associate degrees had median incomes of $761 per week, whereas those who earned a bachelor's degree from a four-year college or university earned a median income of $1,025

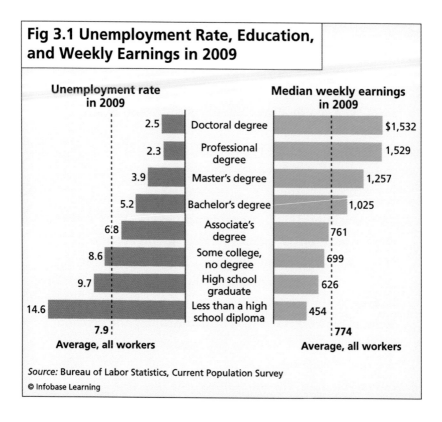

Fig 3.1 Unemployment Rate, Education, and Weekly Earnings in 2009

Unemployment rate in 2009 | Median weekly earnings in 2009

Unemployment rate in 2009	Education	Median weekly earnings in 2009
2.5	Doctoral degree	$1,532
2.3	Professional degree	1,529
3.9	Master's degree	1,257
5.2	Bachelor's degree	1,025
6.8	Associate's degree	761
8.6	Some college, no degree	699
9.7	High school graduate	626
14.6	Less than a high school diploma	454
7.9	Average, all workers	774

Source: Bureau of Labor Statistics, Current Population Survey
© Infobase Learning

per week. Note that earning a college degree means that the median income is 2.25 times higher when compared to those who did not finish high school. Those who complete a master's degree earn median incomes of $1,257 per week, over two times as much as those who graduate from high school but do not attend college. The median salaries increase to $1,529 and $1,532 for professional degrees and doctoral degrees. Each successively higher level of education is associated with a higher level of income.

It is clear from this table that there is a positive, direct relationship between increased education and increased income. Of course, when looking at statistics that report overall averages or medians, it is important to realize that there you cannot accurately predict what your actual personal income will be from these figures. The figures presented are expected amounts based on incomes for large groups of people, but do not account for individual differences. People with similar levels of education may make different amounts of income for many reasons including job experience, age, and the region of the country where you live. However, on average and in general, more education results in higher income.

Additional data from the U.S. Census Bureau (www. USCensus.gov) show that the income advantage of completing college and earning an advanced degree has increased over time. Further, incomes of high school dropouts, who have the least amount of formal education, have fallen when compared to those with more education. Recent changes in technology have created jobs that require more educated workers, so those without education and skills have harder times finding jobs at all and are more likely to be unemployed.

The table at left also shows that there is a clear relationship between education levels and unemployment rates. The more education workers receive, the less likely they are to be unemployed. Those who drop out of high school were almost three times as likely to be unemployed in 2009 (14.6 percent) compared to those who graduated from college (5.2 percent.) Those with master's degrees, professional degrees, and doctoral degrees were least likely to be unemployed, with unemployment rates for all of these groups at under 4 percent. High school dropouts are by far the most likely to be unemployed. Finishing high school reduces the likelihood of being unemployed to less than 10 percent, and attending some college to less than 9 percent. Those who finish college with associate degrees or higher have unemployment rates that are lower than the average for all workers.

Education and Overall Lifetime Earnings

Although we see from the previous table that weekly earnings increase (and unemployment decreases) with more education, we also saw in chapter 2 that there are significant costs to education, both in terms of dollars spent and opportunity costs. Are the overall benefits to you greater than the costs? Although the answer to this question may vary from person to person, one way to address the question is to look at expected lifetime earnings for different levels of education. Information relating lifetime earnings and education from a 2002 study by the U.S. Census Bureau is shown in the following table. Data refer to full-time, year-round workers.

Table 3.2 shows that those who attend some college can expect to have 50 percent higher earnings over their lifetime—an additional half million dollars—when compared to incomes of those who drop out of high school. Those who graduate from high school can expect to have 20 percent more income over their lifetime compared to someone who drops out. Earning a bachelor's degree (a four-year college degree) more than doubles lifetime earnings compared to dropping out of high school, and results in lifetime earnings that are 75 percent ($900,000) higher than lifetime earnings of high school graduates. Lifetime earnings continue to increase with advanced degrees from college—master's degrees, professional degrees, and doctoral degrees. Those with professional degrees such as doctors and lawyers can expect to have the highest lifetime earnings. When we take into account the increases in expected lifetime earnings for college graduates, it is clear that on average and for most people, the increases in incomes will cover the costs of education many times over.

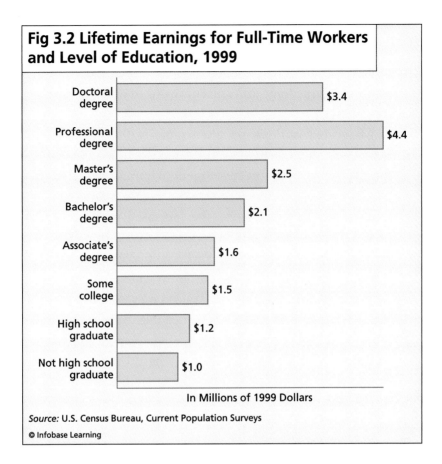

Fig 3.2 Lifetime Earnings for Full-Time Workers and Level of Education, 1999

Level of Education	Earnings
Doctoral degree	$3.4
Professional degree	$4.4
Master's degree	$2.5
Bachelor's degree	$2.1
Associate's degree	$1.6
Some college	$1.5
High school graduate	$1.2
Not high school graduate	$1.0

In Millions of 1999 Dollars

Source: U.S. Census Bureau, Current Population Surveys

© Infobase Learning

Why Does More Education Lead to Higher Incomes?

The main reason why more education leads to higher incomes has to do with productivity. *Productivity* is defined as output per hour of work. For example, assume that your job is to write research reports. If you can write four pages per hour, you are twice as productive as someone who can write two pages per hour. Productivity can increase because of skills obtained on-the-job as well as from skills obtained from school and work effort. In general, if you can increase your productivity you will be on your way to increasing your income. Studies about differences in wages among people throughout time show that large wage differences are due to differences in productivity.

Educated workers are often more skilled than less educated workers who have the same job. The increased productivity from more investment in human capital explains the wage differences between high school graduates and college graduates. The increased productivity may be due to skills and knowledge learned in college, or it may exist because people who go to college are different from people who do not go to college. A person who is unmotivated and unorganized may not be able to meet deadlines. Someone who is not able to focus on assignments will have a hard time being accepted to most colleges and if accepted, will have a hard time graduating. Therefore it may be that the characteristics that make people successful in college also make people successful in the workforce, even if the course work completed in college is not directly related to the job. For example, someone who majored in art history in college may be a productive customer-service representative, even though this job has nothing to do with art history. An employer in a field not related to the arts may be willing to hire the college graduate with a degree in art history because graduating from college signals that the person has the characteristics to be a productive worker.

Education and Lifetime Earnings by Sex and Race

Research has shown that the benefits to education in terms of expected lifetime earnings are different for men

According to the Bureau of Labor Statistics, women earned 89 percent as much as men among workers aged 25 to 34. *(Shutterstock)*

and women and for different racial groups of the population. Men tend to earn more than women throughout their lifetimes for all levels of education, even when they are in the same occupations. Although reasons for these differences in earnings are controversial, some have suggested that women are paid less because they leave and reenter the labor force more often than men due to family responsibilities. Others suggest that women may choose to enter professions that are traditionally lower-paying, such as teaching. Discrimination is also a suggested reason for the pay differences between men and women with the same education levels. However, recent evidence shows that women's incomes are catching up to men's for those who have attended some college or received bachelor's degrees or higher (2010 Bureau of Labor Statistics). Incomes for women who have not attended college or who have less than a high school diploma continue to fall behind those of their male counterparts.

Income earned may also vary significantly by race or Hispanic origin, even accounting for the level of education achieved. The following graph shows average expected lifetime earnings for six different levels of education for non-Hispanic whites, blacks, Asian and Pacific Islanders, and Hispanics, who may be of any race. For most education levels, whites earn more than others with similar educations, and blacks and Hispanics earn less. As with the male–female wage differences not explained by differences in education and skills, suggested reasons for the differences in earnings sometimes point to discrimination and may call for government affirmative action programs. Some differences may also be due to the type of occupation chosen or available, as some occupations pay higher salaries than others due to supply and demand for workers. Other causes of wage differences by race and ethnicity may be due to regional salary differences, to the quality of the schools attended, and to the choice of the major field of study. For example, those with degrees in history generally earn less than those with degrees in engineering.

Although there are earnings differences on average between men and women and among people of different races and ethnicities, it is important to point out that for all groups, on average more education leads to more earnings. For both men and women, the more education

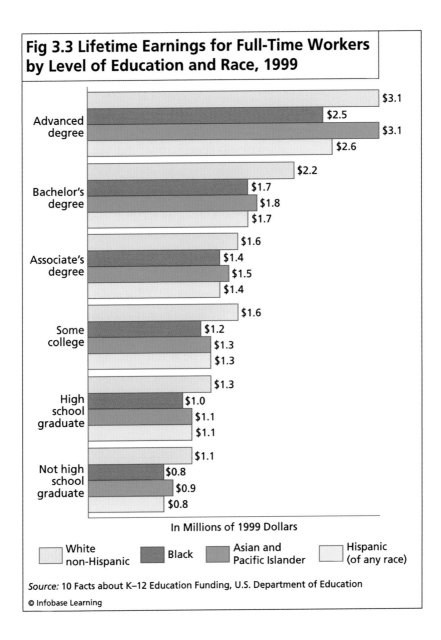

Fig 3.3 Lifetime Earnings for Full-Time Workers by Level of Education and Race, 1999

Advanced degree
- $3.1
- $2.5
- $3.1
- $2.6

Bachelor's degree
- $2.2
- $1.7
- $1.8
- $1.7

Associate's degree
- $1.6
- $1.4
- $1.5
- $1.4

Some college
- $1.6
- $1.2
- $1.3
- $1.3

High school graduate
- $1.3
- $1.0
- $1.1
- $1.1

Not high school graduate
- $1.1
- $0.8
- $0.9
- $0.8

In Millions of 1999 Dollars

- White non-Hispanic
- Black
- Asian and Pacific Islander
- Hispanic (of any race)

Source: 10 Facts about K–12 Education Funding, U.S. Department of Education

© Infobase Learning

the higher the income. And for all races and ethnicities, more education leads to higher incomes.

Personal Benefits of Education in Addition to Increased Income

Although increased expected earnings are important, there is more to life than money. Education provides many personal benefits in addition to increased income. With a college education or job-specific training, you will likely qualify for a more rewarding and more challenging job than if you are an unskilled worker. Your overall job satisfaction will likely be higher. Since you will likely spend a good portion of your life on the job, having a worthwhile and gratifying career can be an important benefit of education.

To find out about other benefits to education, ask someone who has graduated from college if they would do it all over again and if they would recommend college to others. The answer is likely to be a resounding YES. Ask them what was so good about college in addition to preparing them for a more challenging and higher paying job, and the answers are likely to fall into several categories.

First, most two- and four-year college degree programs in the United States require and encourage you to study a wide range of subjects in addition to your major. For example, assume that you plan to major in chemistry in college. Despite this specific interest, your college may require you to take courses in arts and humanities, social sciences, physical education, mathematics, and a foreign language in addition to chemistry courses. This broad-based education opens your eyes to many areas of study and gives you an opportunity to learn about many things as well as chemistry. Those foreign language courses may increase your appreciation for and enjoyment from foreign travel. Those art and music courses may provide you more enjoyment from visiting museums and attending concerts. The political science and economics courses may help you to understand current events and help you to make more sense of the world around you.

Second, a college education (and advanced degrees) from an accredited school gives you a certain amount of prestige. Being a college graduate tells the world that you have been successful in completing something very important. You have the ability to finish what you started, to manage your time and resources, to solve problems, and to pass exams. You show that you can play by the rules and that you have successfully studied many subjects and passed many courses. A college degree gives people self-confidence and self-esteem. Graduating from college is a major accomplishment and signals to others that you are an achiever.

Another major benefit of continuing your education through college and beyond is that knowledge can be an end in itself. It feels good when you know and understand things. Your college education can expand your mind and serve as an introduction to the world of ideas. You may be better able to understand many of the phenomena around you—the weather, the world's religions, earthquakes, and the importance of history. You will be able to better appreciate and enjoy literature, art, music, and cultural diversity. The more you learn, the more you are likely to love learning. Studying at a college or university teaches you how to learn and how to keep finding new information. Many people report that attending college instilled in them a life-long love of learning. The knowledge you acquire in college is not the end of learning, but the beginning of continuing to learn throughout your life.

Another personal benefit from continuing your education is that for many people, college is fun. Going to classes, reading, meeting professors and other students

Personal Benefits of a College Education

Higher expected income

Less chance of being unemployed

More rewarding and challenging career

Opportunity for learning in many areas

Prestige

Greater understanding of world around you

Increase enjoyment from learning throughout lifetime

Enjoyment—Having fun!

can all be rewarding and different from other things you have done and will do with your life. Many colleges and universities give you opportunities to get involved in student organizations, where you can make friends who share your interests. You will also meet people in your classes and through alumni networking organizations after you graduate. Many college graduates report that making life-long friends and having continuing social networking opportunities is an important advantage of getting a college education.

EXTERNAL BENEFITS OF EDUCATION

We mentioned earlier that there are external benefits to education in addition to personal benefits. We will now look at external benefits in more detail. Usually if you consume something, the benefits of that consumption go to you. For example, if you consume fruit and yogurt for breakfast, you are the one who derives the benefits from consuming the food. The producer or supplier of the fruit and yogurt also derive benefits from selling the food. Usually benefits stop with the consumer and producer or seller of the product. However, sometimes when you consume something others may benefit also, even when they are not buyers or sellers of the product. Education is an example where external benefits exist. External benefits are sometimes called positive externalities.

External benefits exist if the actions of one person make another person better off, and when that other person is not the buyer or seller of the product. With respect to education, if you decide to stay in school longer, you will benefit personally by having higher earnings and in the other ways discussed in the last section. But others benefit when people get educated, too. For example, since more education leads to less unemployment, educated people are less likely to be poor and to need public as-

External Benefits of Education

Education leads to:

Higher literacy rates and fewer traffic accidents

Less unemployment and less need for public assistance

More informed citizenry and greater voter participation rates

Improved health, including fewer smokers

Lower crime rates

More volunteers to help others and more blood donors

More research

Source: www.collegeboard.com/prod_downloads/press/cost04/
EducationPays2004.pdf

According to the U.S. Census Bureau, 63.6 percent of men and women 18 years and over voted in November of 2008. *(Shutterstock)*

sistance. This benefits taxpayers, whose taxes could be reduced or whose tax dollars could go to pay for other programs.

Education provides other important external benefits. People who can read and write and make good decisions about current issues can be more informed voters and better citizens. Studies have shown that those who graduate from college are more likely to vote than those who are not college graduates. It is important for democracies to have educated voters who understand current issues. People who are educated are better able to teach their children to read and write and to teach their children to value education, so the benefits get passed on through generations.

Education also has external benefits related to health. Educated people are better able to understand things about public health like the importance of sanitation, nutrition, and vaccinations and to pass this knowledge on to others, thus reducing disease. College graduates are much less likely to take up smoking than those with less education, and this reduces the negative effects of smoking on others, such as effects of second-hand smoke.

Educated people are also less likely to commit serious crimes and to be sent to prison, which benefits both potential crime victims and also saves taxpayer money on incarceration expenses. Increased education is also associated with doing good things to help others. College graduates are over four times more likely to volunteer to help others when compared to high school dropouts, and also volunteer for more hours each year. College graduates are almost three times more likely to donate blood than high school dropouts.

Another external benefit related to education comes from research. If a research scientist discovers the cure for a disease, he or she will reap some of the benefits through salary and benefits. But others benefit also, because other people benefit from not getting sick. Research into computers and the Internet has increased communication and access to information throughout the world. Research resulting in improved transportation has led to increased trade throughout the world, giving people access to more and different types of goods and services.

If only the private benefits of education are taken into account, less education would be demanded than if the external benefits are also taken into account. For example, when you decide how much education you will pursue, you will logically consider the benefits to you and not the external benefits. But because there are external benefits to education as well as private benefits, governments often choose to provide subsidies to education to encourage more education. In the United States, this is done by providing free public schools through high school, and by providing public colleges and universities where the tuition and fees that students pay are much lower than the total cost of the education. As we saw in chapter 2, the government also provides scholarships and low-interest loans to college students. Governments also promote education by setting rules requiring students to stay in school until they reach certain ages and by providing tax breaks for some education-related expenses.

Education and Economic Development

Related to external benefits, education is important to help poor countries develop their economies and to raise people out of poverty. The more capital and technology a country has, the easier it is to produce goods and services for people in the country. As an economic resource, *capital* refers to factories, machinery, tools, and equipment used to produce goods and services. *Technology* refers to things that increase the output of goods and services from the amount of workers and capital available. Examples of technology are the printing press, the telephone, computers, and the Internet. When people are able to use capital and technology to produce more goods and services, these goods and services can be used by people in the country or exported to other countries in exchange for imports or money. In either case the increased production means that more people have jobs and are earning income.

More educated workers are more productive and help economies to grow. Productivity is tied to economic growth, and economic growth is tied to increases in income and standards of living in countries throughout the world. Rich countries have higher overall productivity and poor countries have lower overall productivity. Increases in education and training increase worker productivity, and are also a source of technological advancement. People who develop better computers, for example, have to have special skills and knowledge to be able to do this. Technological advancement then leads to increased productivity for other workers.

For people to be able to use technology, they have to have skills and education. For example, medical technology for performing surgery requires skilled doctors and medical technicians. For countries that are already behind in economic development, the failure to emphasize education will hurt their ability to catch up with other countries. To help people in the poorest countries of the world, improving the quality of education and access to education is critically important.

Summary

Education has many benefits to both individuals and to society. More education brings higher incomes and lowers the likelihood of being unemployed. The expected lifetime income of a college graduate is 1.75 times higher than that of a high school graduate, and 2.1 times higher than that of a high school dropout. There are other personal benefits to education as well, including access to more rewarding jobs, and increased knowledge and ability to understand the world around you. In deciding whether or not to continue your education, you want to compare your expected costs to your expected benefits over your lifetime.

There are external benefits to education as well, including reduced crime, more educated citizens, more volunteerism, and factors leading to improved health. For developing countries, education leading to increased worker productivity is important for economic growth. The external benefits to education provide a rationale for the government to encourage and promote education through providing public schools and universities, through tax incentives, and by providing scholarships and low-interest loans for college students.

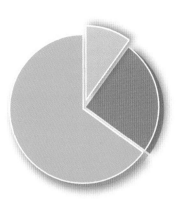

4

Planning for the Future: Your Education

If you decide that the benefits of continuing your education are worth the costs, you now have other important decisions to make. You have to decide what type of college to attend and then choose a college that suits you. Related to this is deciding what to specialize in or major in college. Your major is the subject or area in which you specialize. For some students, choosing the right college may be easy: You may have always wanted to attend your state university, you can afford it, you know you have the grades and test scores to be admitted, and you know it offers the academic programs that you want. But for other students, the decision may not be so straightforward. Should you go to a vocational school, a community college, or a four-year college or university? Should you consider both public and private schools? What size school is best for you? Would you prefer to stay in-state or go out-of-state? Would you prefer to be in a city or in a more rural environment? The College Board, a nonprofit organization with the mission of helping students achieve college success, suggests that you consider these and other criteria when deciding on a college (www.collegesearch. collegeboard.com.) This chapter will discuss factors you may want to consider in choosing a college. It will also discuss the application process for four-year colleges and choosing a college major.

VOCATIONAL, TWO-YEAR, OR FOUR-YEAR COLLEGE?

In chapter 1, we discussed some differences between vocational schools, community colleges or two-year colleges, and four-year colleges and universities. We will now review some of these differences and look at these types of institutions in the context of choosing the type of institution that is best for you. Choosing the right type of school may depend on your career goals, which will be discussed in chapter 5.

Vocational Schools

Some jobs require specific licenses and training but do not require or expect you to have a four-year college degree. If you are a high school graduate who is interested in a specific skilled job such as being an electronics technician, a hair stylist, a truck driver, or a medical assistant, a vocational school may be right for you. Vocational schools go by a variety of names including technical schools, trade schools, and career schools or colleges. The word *vocation* means the specific career for which you are trained, and this is where vocational schools get their names. The purpose of vocational schools is to train you

According to the National Center for Education Statistics, there were 1,200 area Career/Technical Education (CTE) schools in 41 states in 2002. *(Shutterstock)*

for a specific job rather than offering more broad-based course work and opportunities to learn other subjects. Attending a vocational school can be a means to qualify for a skilled job or trade that you may enjoy for a long time.

In some cases, attending a vocational school can also be an important step toward furthering your career in the future. Some vocational schools have programs where some courses transfer to two-year or four-year colleges and universities. In these cases, studying in a vocational school could lead to a skilled job now and then later be a step toward completing a college degree. For example, you could go to a vocational school to become a medical

Why Choose a Vocational or Trade School?

1. Career-oriented training
2. Good for those who have a specific career plan for a skilled trade
3. Easily make the transition from school to career
4. Takes less time to prepare for career than other types of higher education
5. Many different vocational programs and course offerings available
6. May include hands-on training as well as classroom and online learning

assistant and then later return to college to earn a four-year degree and become a registered nurse.

In addition to offering career-oriented training, vocational schools frequently require less time than two- or four-year colleges. The training that you get and the courses you take will focus on your career goal, and may include hands-on training or apprenticeships in work environments to give you job experience.

Community Colleges

A community college can be an excellent way to begin your higher education, whether your goal is to earn a vocational certificate or license for a specific job or to earn an associate degree in two years and then transfer to a four-year college or university. Community colleges, also called junior colleges, are usually publically funded institutions. They are located throughout the country, usually in areas where it is easy to drive or to reach by public transportation. They sometimes partner with local businesses and focus on the needs of those in their local communities.

The mission of community colleges is to provide low-cost education to people in the community where they are located. Tuition in community colleges is usually lower than for other types of education, and financial aid programs are available. They have "open-access" admissions policies, meaning that you do not need high grades or test scores to be admitted and attend classes. Community colleges frequently have agreements with four-year colleges and universities in their states to make transferring easy for students who have completed an associate degree.

The flexibility of taking courses at community colleges is appealing to many students. They offer full-time and part-time programs and offer courses for credit and

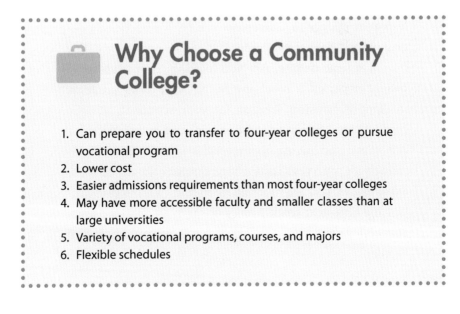

Why Choose a Community College?

1. Can prepare you to transfer to four-year colleges or pursue vocational program
2. Lower cost
3. Easier admissions requirements than most four-year colleges
4. May have more accessible faculty and smaller classes than at large universities
5. Variety of vocational programs, courses, and majors
6. Flexible schedules

not-for-credit. If you are not fully committed to going to college for two or four full years, you can enroll in a course or two at a community college and see how it goes. Community colleges also welcome adult students who wish to continue their education later in life.

Community colleges vary a great deal according to the local community in which they are located and include both small rural colleges and large urban colleges. They also vary in the types of programs and certificates offered, but generally offer a wide assortment of courses, vocational certificates, and degree programs. Community college faculty are hired to be teachers and do not have the research or publishing responsibilities that instructors in four-year colleges often have. Classes may be smaller when compared to large lecture sections at some four-year colleges and universities.

Four-Year Colleges and Universities

Should you go to a four-year college or university for all four years? Many students choose this option. There are many reasons for doing so. When you graduate from a four-year college or university, you have a bachelor's degree, which is what most people mean when they say they have a college degree. Are you looking for a traditional college experience involving living with other students in campus housing, rooting for your school in athletic competitions, joining campus social and extracurricular programs, and having opportunities to study abroad? Although all four-year institutions do not offer all of these experiences, you are more likely to find these opportunities at a four-year institution. For many people, the four-year college experience is something they would not want to miss.

Many students prefer to have the four-year experience of staying at one school rather than transferring from a community college. Staying four years in one place gives them more time to get to know their fellow students and professors. They have more continuity in their course-work without concerns about transferring credits. Most four-year colleges and universities offer well-rounded educations where students study a variety of subjects in addition to their areas of specialization, and most offer a wide variety of possible majors from which to choose.

Recall from chapter 3 that earning a college degree greatly increases your likelihood of earning more money over your lifetime. This is in part because a college degree prepares you for specific higher-level jobs that pay higher salaries. But it is also because completing your college degree signals to employers that you have a broad-based education and skills and competencies that apply to many occupations. Earning a bachelor's degree is also a necessary step if you plan to attend graduate school in the future.

Why Choose a Four-Year College or University?

1. Leads to bachelor's degree
2. Traditional college experience
3. Well-rounded education
4. Variety of courses and majors
5. Prepares for higher level jobs and higher salaries
6. Prepares for graduate school

Decision-making: Type of College

The following table provides a decision-making grid that may be helpful in deciding whether to attend a vocational school, a community or two-year college, or a four-year college or university. The first column lists the three alternatives. The top row lists different criteria you may wish to consider in making your choice. Of course, you need to decide what criteria are important to you, and list those criteria in your own decision-making grid. Your criteria may include things like the length of time the program will take, the prestige of the degree, the enjoyment you anticipate receiving while attending the college, and so on.

Once you decide what criteria are important to you, you should rank your criteria in order of importance. For example, if low cost is the most important criteria to you, you would put this in the second column. If preparing for a specific job—for example, law enforcement—is the next most important criterion to you, you would list this next,

DECISION-MAKING GRID: WHAT TYPE OF COLLEGE SHOULD YOU ATTEND?

(POSSIBLE) CRITERIA → ALTERNATIVES ↓	Low cost	Prepares you for a specific career	Leads to bachelor's degree	Variety of courses
Vocational School				
Two-year College				
Four-year College				

and so on. After you have listed and ranked your criteria, you want to evaluate whether each type of school meets the criteria. You can do this with plusses and minuses. If a private vocational school is expensive, you would put a minus sign in the box corresponding to "vocational school" and "low cost." If your state university is both inexpensive and has degrees in criminal justice leading to a career in law enforcement, you would put plus signs in the corresponding boxes. Although using the decision-making grid is not an exact science, seeing the overall plusses and minuses may help you to make your decision.

Choosing the Right College or University

After you choose what level of education you wish to pursue, your next decision involves choosing a college that is right for you. Some of the same considerations apply to choosing a vocational school, a community college, or a four-year college or university and these are listed on the next page. For example, in all cases you want to find a school where you will be happy and successful, that you can afford, and that meets your educational and career goals. You also want to make sure that the school is reputable and accredited by the appropriate agency. However, some considerations apply specifically to vocational schools, community colleges, or four-year colleges and universities, so we will look at some of these considerations now.

Choosing a Vocational School

There are many vocational schools in existence in the United States, and like all schools, the quality of programs and costs can vary greatly. Vocational schools can be public (supported by government funding) or private. For-profit private schools rely on student fees to cover their expenses, so they depend on enrollments to

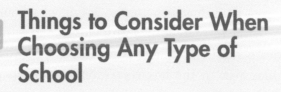

Things to Consider When Choosing Any Type of School

Will you be happy?

Can you succeed?

Can you afford it?

Does it meet your educational goals and offer the programs you want?

Does it meet your potential career goals?

Is it accredited by the appropriate agency?

earn profits. Although many private vocational schools are honest and prepare students for the jobs they promise, others may mislead students and not be able to follow through on their promises. In a publication called *Choosing a Career or Vocational School,* the Federal Trade Commission (FTC) recommends that you exercise caution when considering a private vocational school. The FTC is a government agency whose job is to protect consumers from fraudulent business practices.

If you are considering enrolling in a private vocational school, it is important that you investigate the school before paying any money or signing a contract. The sidebar on the next page summarizes some of the suggestions from the FTC about choosing a vocational school. It is important to investigate if the school is licensed or accredited, and by whom. Private vocational schools are often licensed by state agencies through the Department of Education. Make sure the accrediting agency is reputable. If you are able to get comparable training through a community college, this will be less expensive and may otherwise be a better choice.

You should visit the school, sit in on a class or two, and talk to current students. Ask about the qualifications of instructors. Ask about the success of the school in placing students in jobs. Contact people who graduated from the program and ask them about their experiences. Ask about the total cost of the program, including tuition, fees, uniforms, books, and so on. For-profit vocational schools can be very expensive. In a 2010 article, the *New York Times* reported that tuition in for-profit trade schools can be very high. After graduating, wages may not be as high as promised by recruiters, so students end up with large debts that are difficult to repay. Check with consumer protection agencies to see if complaints have been filed against the school.

Things to Consider When Choosing a Private Vocational School

Is it accredited or licensed by the appropriate agency?

Can you get the same training at a community college?

Visit the school and ask to sit in on classes.

Ask about the success rate of the program.

Ask for names of recent graduates, and contact them for information.

Ask about the total cost of the program and financial aid.

Check with the Better Business Bureau and Attorney General's office in your state.

Choosing a Community College

If you decide that a community college is the best choice for you, you may choose to attend the college in your local community since it is most convenient. However if you live in an area where you have more than one option available, or if you are considering attending a community college in a different area, then you may want to consider other factors in addition to convenience. There may be differences in the types of courses, certificates and programs offered. There may be differences in times and frequency of course offerings, or in online course offerings. One college may have different sports programs or student organizations.

Probably your principle concern in choosing the best community college for you has to do with your future goals. If you are going to a community college to learn specific job skills, you want to locate the best program for your future career. If you are going to a community college for two years and then plan to transfer to a four-year college or university, you want to find a community college that will help you transfer credits to the school you plan to attend in the future. If you already have a four-year college in mind, find out if any community colleges have special transfer programs with that college.

Choosing a Four-Year College or University

There are many different options in four-year colleges and universities with respect to size, location, tuition and fees, and areas of specialization. Finding the one that is best for you may involve asking yourself some questions about your preferences, goals, and resources. There are Web sites from reputable organizations that are designed to help you search for colleges and universities that meet your preferences. For example, you may want to look at the Web sites of the College Board, the ACT, the Princeton Review, or www.college.gov. You should visit college Web sites for information, but also try to visit colleges and universities in person. Take organized tours and talk to current students. Attend college fairs and talk to college recruiters.

Considering your personal goals for college is an important first step in this process. For example, if you hope to study fashion merchandising in college, you want to make sure that you find a school that offers courses in that field. Do not think, however, that you need to know exactly what you want to study in college and what your career goals are to make a good choice about what school to attend. Many students form goals and recognize new interests when they are in college. If you hope to participate in a certain sport in college, you want to make sure that you find a school that has programs in that sport. In

Things to Consider When Choosing a Four-Year College or University

1. What are your goals for college?
2. Will you be accepted?
3. Large or small?
4. Class size and accessible faculty?
5. Cost?
6. Public or private?
7. Athletic and social programs?
8. Location?
9. Campus environment and housing?
10. Reputation?

addition to differences in course content and programs, there are four-year colleges with connections to specific religions, for women, and with traditionally black student bodies. Assessing your goals and interests may help you to narrow your choices.

It is important to realize that four-year colleges and universities have different admissions requirements and that all students will not be accepted to all four-year colleges and universities. Admission is often competitive and based on your high school grade point average, test scores, high school activities, and community service. As you begin to narrow your college choices, investigate admissions requirements and make sure you are within the realistic range of being accepted to schools you are considering so you will not be disappointed.

The size of four-year colleges and universities usually refers to how many students are enrolled, and this varies greatly. There are colleges with fewer than 1,000 students enrolled, and colleges with over 35,000 students enrolled. Some students prefer to attend a large university because of a wider variety of course offerings, sports and social programs, living arrangements, and research opportunities. On the other hand, some students believe they will get lost in the crowd at a large university. Courses are sometimes taught by graduate students, and some lecture sections may have hundreds of students enrolled. Some students may wish to have more individual attention that a smaller school may provide.

The cost of higher education is often one of the most important factors in a student's decision about which college to attend. Costs vary a great deal, with public in-state universities usually being less expensive than out-of-state public schools or private schools. However, as discussed in chapter 2, you should not reject a college because its

According to the National Center for Education Statistics, the cost of undergraduate tuition, room, and board at public institutions rose 32 percent between 1999 and 2009. *(Shutterstock)*

advertised cost is too high without looking into available financial aid. Some schools that appear to be expensive provide significant assistance to students in need.

Public and private colleges and universities can both be large or small, can both provide financial aid, and can both be prestigious. Because they do not rely on government funding, private schools have more discretion in who they can admit and in focusing on topics such as religion. Private schools often advertise smaller classes and more individual attention from professors. Large public universities may have more options for housing, especially for freshmen.

For some students, the athletic and social programs offered by the college are an important part of the college experience. Some students like to participate in or attend highly publicized sports events and therefore prefer schools in major athletic conferences. Others may wish to be in a less competitive environment and may prefer a school with more casual intramural programs. Some students look forward to joining a social fraternity or sorority, whereas other students may prefer schools where most students do not join these organizations.

Location and housing can be important factors in choosing a college or university. Will you commute to campus or live on campus? Do you want to be close to home or far from home? Do you want to be in a large city or in a more rural environment? Do you want to live in a dormitory that serves food or in an apartment where you can cook for yourself? If you have strong preferences about location and housing, investigate the options available to you at schools you are considering.

The reputation of your college or university can be important in many ways. For the rest of your life, you will be a graduate of this school. Some students want to attend the best college to which they can be admitted. There are several organizations that rate or rank colleges and universities, such as *U.S. News and World Report* and Princeton Review. When looking at ratings, it is important to look at what goes into the rating system. For example, part of the rating system may be based on having small classes. If small classes are not important to you, you may not agree with the overall rankings. If you are considering a private college that is not well-established, be sure that the school is accredited by a reputable accrediting agency. You do not want to invest a lot of time and money and then find that your degree is not respected by graduate schools or employers.

APPLYING TO A FOUR-YEAR COLLEGE OR UNIVERSITY

The application process to four-year colleges and universities is often more involved than the process to apply to vocational schools or community colleges, so it helps to be aware of what applications may include. The college application process has undergone major changes in the past several years. Whereas applications used to be primarily filled out by hand and mailed, now they are often submitted online. It is increasingly possible to submit one online application to multiple schools, saving you much time and effort. But it is important for you to find out the requirements for the schools in which you are interested and to follow the procedures precisely. Several reputable organizations including the College Board and Embark. com have detailed college application advice on their Web sites. We will summarize some of this advice here.

How Many Schools?

Many experts suggest that you narrow your choices to about five to eight colleges. If you have researched schools and thought carefully about your preferences and the different options that may work for you, applying to 20 or more colleges may not make sense. Application fees can also be expensive. You may wish to divide your schools into different categories. For example, maybe you would like to attend an elite Ivy League college, but you are not certain if you would be accepted. You may want to apply to one or two such "reach" schools. You should also apply to schools where you are reasonably sure that you will be admitted and that you are reasonably sure that you can afford. These could be your "regular" schools. You should also include some schools where you are very certain you will be admitted. These could be your "safe" schools.

If you are very sure what your first-choice college is, you may want to find out if it has an early decision program. In addition to regular admission application deadlines, some schools have earlier application deadlines for students who know that a school is their first choice. Usually if you apply and are accepted in an early decision type of program, you commit to attend that school and then would not need to apply to other schools.

What Do Applications Include?

In most cases, you need to provide your high school transcript, standardized test scores, letters of recommendation, and personal essays when you apply to a college. An interview may be required. You may also apply for financial aid when you apply for admission. Check with the schools where you plan to apply for specific information and deadlines for each part of your application. If the application deadline is in the fall of your senior year, you may also need to send in a mid-year grade report. Some schools require scores on the SAT (Scholastic Aptitude Test) and some require scores on the ACT (American College Test.) If you have taken Advanced Placement exams, you may also need to submit those scores. Pay close attention to test dates and college submission deadlines. Some students find it worthwhile to take practice exams or test preparation courses before taking the ACT or the SAT. You can check the exam Web sites for practice test information (http://sat.collegeboard.com; www.actstudent. org).

If letters of recommendation are required for the schools where you are applying, be sure to give your references enough time to write the letters for you. One month is a good length of time. Choose people who know you well and can speak to your strengths to write the letters. For high school students, this would usually be a teacher, coach, or guidance counselor. Be sure to thank those who write letters for you.

Many applications require personal essays, which help college admissions officers get to know you better. Be sure to give yourself enough time to do a good job on these essays. Ask people to read them over for you, to check for mistakes, and also check to make sure that the message in your essay is clear and organized. Some schools also require personal interviews of prospective students, either with university personnel at the college or with alumni who live in your area. The College Board Web site has an interview checklist and interview advice, as well as advice on writing college essays. Do not forget to thank the person who interviews you.

If you are applying for a scholarship or financial aid, your scholarship or financial aid application may be part of your overall application for admission. Some schools will inform you of a financial aid package when you are admitted. Be sure to find out the procedure for applying for financial aid and other financial awards at the schools where you are applying.

CHOOSING YOUR COLLEGE MAJOR

An important decision that you will make some time in your college career is what your major will be. Your major affects the type of degree that you earn and the course work that you take. For example, if you major in history you will take more courses in history than in other subjects and will earn a B.A. (Bachelor of Arts) degree in history. You will likely be required to satisfy requirements for the history major by taking a series of specific

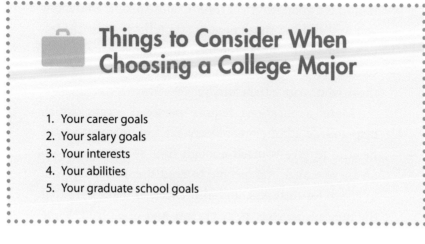

Things to Consider When Choosing a College Major

1. Your career goals
2. Your salary goals
3. Your interests
4. Your abilities
5. Your graduate school goals

history courses, and you would also have some elective courses from which to choose. If you major in chemistry, you would take a series of required and elective courses in chemistry and related sciences, and would graduate with a B.S. (Bachelor of Science) degree in chemistry. In some cases you may be able to major in two subjects (have a double major.) You may also be able to choose one or more minors. A *minor* is also an area of specialization but with less required course work than for a major.

When you begin attending a college or university or even before, you will be asked many times about your major. However, in most cases you do not have to make this decision right away. And many students change their major when they discover an interesting new area or when they discover where their academic strengths lie. Because you will take a variety of courses to satisfy requirements in your first two years of college, you have an opportunity to sample different subjects before you commit to a specific major. Many schools do not ask you to declare your major until the end of your sophomore year. If you earn an associate's degree from a two-year college and then transfer to a four-year school, you will probably declare your major when you transfer.

For many students, the choice of a college major relates to the choice of a future career, which will be discussed in chapter 5. For example, if you think you want to be an engineer, you would major in engineering in college. If you think you want to be a high school English

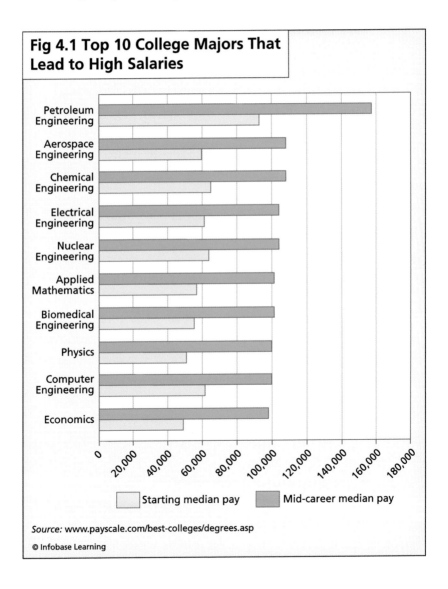

Fig 4.1 Top 10 College Majors That Lead to High Salaries

Source: www.payscale.com/best-colleges/degrees.asp

© Infobase Learning

teacher, you would determine the requirements to earn a teaching credential in your state and you would probably major in English or education. If you have a clear career goal, you should investigate what education you need to reach that goal. This may help you decide what your major should be. In some cases, however, the choice of a college major is not related to a specific career. Many majors prepare you for a variety of careers.

Your choice of a college major and your resulting career choice also affects your future salary. A 2010 report by PayScale.com lists college majors and starting and mid-career median pay for people with bachelor's degrees and no higher degrees. The graph on page 77 shows the 10 college majors that their study concludes lead to the highest salaries. Seven of the top 10 highest paying college majors are in engineering. Although high starting and future salaries may be important, there are other considerations in choosing a college major. Your interests and your abilities are also important.

From their high school experiences, some students develop strong interests in learning more in a certain subject relating to the sciences or the arts, for example. Others may know that they want to study foreign languages or the social sciences. Your aptitude for certain subjects may also affect your choice of a major. For example, you may begin thinking that you want to major in political science to prepare for a legal career and later discover that you do better in mathematics courses. This may lead you to change your major to a subject with a more quantitative focus.

If you plan to go to graduate school after you earn a bachelor's degree, you may want to check to see what is required for the graduate program in which you hope to enroll. For example, if you want to be a medical doctor, you might check with a medical school to see what course work you would need in your bachelor's degree program to be accepted to medical school. If you want to be a lawyer, you might check with a law school to see what type of undergraduate preparation they recommend to be accepted to law school.

SUMMARY

Making decisions about your future education is an exciting prospect. Initially you need to decide what type of education is best for you—a vocational school, a community college, or a four-year college or university. Once you make that decision, you can focus on choosing specific schools to which to apply. Many factors can affect your decision, such as size of the school, location, cost, reputation, the experience it offers, and the degree programs available. Carefully follow the procedures for the application process at the schools where you apply. Making decisions about where to apply and eventually choosing a college major can seem overwhelming, but keep in mind that many of these decisions are not irreversible. Many students transfer from one type of college to another, and many students change their college major. If you view education as a lifelong process, your choices and opportunities can continue to evolve.

5

Planning for the Future: Your Career

Planning for your career and finding the right job has important implications for the rest of your life. In some cases, knowing what career you would like to pursue affects your education decisions. In other cases, your education decisions may drive your career choices. Sometimes a general education will prepare you for a variety of jobs.

The availability of jobs depends on many things including the supply of workers in different occupations, the demand for goods and services, how different goods and services are produced, and the overall state of the economy. This chapter will discuss several factors related to choosing a career. We will look at things you may wish to consider in making a career choice and how you can find out about different jobs and career options. We will also discuss the job search, the job application, and the job interview.

ASSESSING YOUR INTERESTS, ABILITIES, AND VALUES

A good way to begin thinking about choosing a career is to think about your interests and what you would like to do in your career. Are you artistic? Are you social? Do you like working with numbers and paying attention to details? Would you like to start a new business? Taking a self-test can be a very helpful way to explore your interests and to think about things that are important to you. Several organizations have developed assessment instruments or self-tests to help you pin down areas of interest and to connect these interests to possible careers. You should be aware that some organizations charge you a fee to take self-tests, but that there are valuable self-tests that are available to you for free. High school and college vocational counselors and career center personnel are often skilled in helping you take these tests to help you identify what type of job may be best for you. These self-tests are not tests with right and wrong answers. They ask you to respond to questions based on your opinions about your interests and things you would like to do. This may help you decide what is important to you in choosing a career.

Your Interests

The U.S. Department of Labor designed one of the best known and most often used self-tests to help you determine your interests and connect your interests to a career. It is called the O*NET Interest Profiler and it is one of several career exploration tools they have made available online. O*NET stands for the Occupational Information Network. O*NET tools are designed to help you both explore options for choosing a career and to help

Sample Statements from O*NET Interest Profiler

Build kitchen cabinets

Write stories or articles for magazines

Help people with personal or emotional problems

Buy and sell stocks and bonds

Keep accounts payable/receivable for an office

Diagnose and treat sick animals

Dance in a Broadway show

Teach children how to play sports

Give a presentation about a product you are selling

Transfer funds between banks using a computer

Source: www.onetcenter.org/IP.html

you prepare for your career. The tools are available online and in print at www.onetcenter.org.

The O*NET Interest Profiler consists of 180 statements describing work activities. To complete the Interest Profiler, you respond "LIKE" if you think you would like doing this activity, "DISLIKE" if you think you would not like doing this activity, and "UNSURE" if you are not sure if you would like the activity or not. The sidebar gives a sample of 10 of the 180 statements on the O*NET Interest Profiler. After you complete and score the entire O*NET assessment, you can determine if your interests fall into one of six categories related to work activities: artistic, conventional, enterprising, investigative, realistic, or social.

According to O*NET, if you have *artistic* interests, you like work activities that deal with forms and designs. You like to express yourself, and may enjoy working in a setting without clear rules. *Conventional* interests mean that you like to follow established procedures and routines. You like working with data and details. *Enterprising* people like to begin and carry out projects, and to persuade people and make decisions. Those with *investigative* interests prefer work activities that deal with ideas. They like to search and figure out problems. If your interests are primarily *realistic,* you like hands-on problems and solutions. You prefer working outside rather than in jobs that require a lot of paperwork. If you have *social* interests, you like helping others and working with others. You prefer communication to working with objects or machines.

After you have thought about your interests in job activities, you can use this information to investigate related

Job Interest Categories

Artistic

Conventional

Enterprising

Investigative

Realistic

Social

Source: www.onetcenter.org/IP.html

careers. O*NET links the six interest categories with over 800 related occupations. Each occupation states which of five different levels of preparation or education is required, ranging from little or no preparation to extensive preparation. For example, a composer is an artistic occupation requiring extensive preparation. A file clerk is a conventional occupation requiring little or no preparation. Human resource managers are enterprising occupations requiring considerable preparation. A food service technician is an investigative occupation requiring some preparation. An electrician is a realistic occupation requiring medium preparation. College economics teacher is a social occupation requiring extensive preparation.

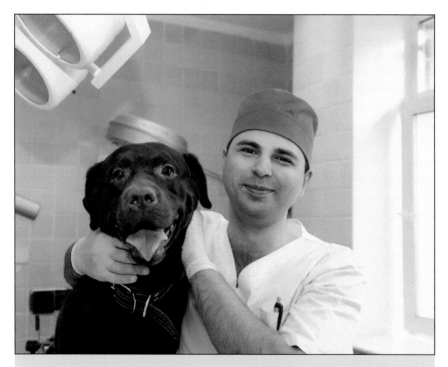

A veterinarian is a demanding occupation requiring extensive preparation. *(Shutterstock)*

Of course there are ways to assess your interests other than using the six categories in the preceding list. You may already know that you would like to work in an office, or with animals, or outdoors, or preparing food, or in agriculture, or alone. Your own preferences may not always be clear from taking a standard self-assessment instrument. And there are many factors to consider in choosing a job other than your interests. For example, your abilities are important and are often related to your level of education, as discussed in chapter 4.

Your Abilities

O'NET offers a free online Ability Profiler that helps you to assess your strengths or abilities in nine areas (www. onetcenter.org/AP.html). The abilities assessed are:

- *Verbal ability
- *Arithmetic reasoning
- *Computation
- *Spatial ability
- *Form perception
- *Clerical perception
- *Motor coordination
- *Finger dexterity
- *Manual dexterity

Strengths in these different areas are then linked to more than 800 occupations. For example, recognizing that you do or do not have strong finger dexterity may influence your decision to pursue a career as a word processor or a surgeon. Recognizing that you do or do not have strong verbal abilities may influence your decision to pursue a career as teacher or a receptionist.

Your Values

In addition to interests and abilities, your values and preferences for different work environments are important considerations in choosing a career. Your work values refer to aspects of work that are important to you. Is having a feeling of accomplishment important to you? Or recognition? Or loyalty from your company and your boss? Do you like to be busy? These are some examples of work values. The sidebar lists six different work values that you may consider in choosing a career. O*NET provides an online Work Importance Locator that helps you to assess these values (www.onetcenter.org/WIL. html). If *achievement* is important to you, you may like a job that lets you use your best abilities and see the results of your efforts. If *independence* is an important value to you, you may like a job where you can make decisions on your own. *Recognition* means that you may like a job with prestige and possibilities for advancement. If you hope to find friendly coworkers and help others, *relationships*

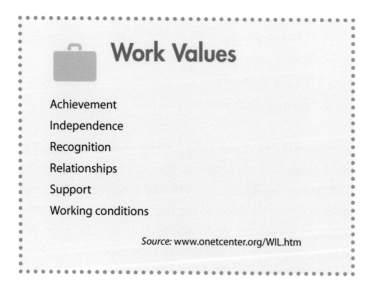

Work Values

Achievement

Independence

Recognition

Relationships

Support

Working conditions

Source: www.onetcenter.org/WIL.htm

are an important value to you. *Support* as a work value means that the company and management support their workers. *Working conditions* refers to a variety of things including pay, job security, benefits, and the working environment. You need to think about which values relating to working conditions are most important to you.

LEARNING ABOUT SPECIFIC OCCUPATIONS

In addition to identifying occupations that correspond to your interests, abilities, and values, you are probably interested in other characteristics of specific occupations. How can you learn about the training and education needed to be a preschool teacher or a carpenter? Where can you find information about the earnings of a registered nurse compared to a licensed vocational nurse? Are job prospects good for chemical engineers? Maybe you think you might like to be a forester but you do not know exactly what you would be doing in this position. Where can you find out what workers actually do in different jobs? What about working conditions and safety factors? Fortunately there is a great source of information to find out about specific jobs. It is the Occupational Outlook Handbook (OOH) of the Bureau of Labor Statistics, a division of the U.S. government (www.bls.gov/oco/). As shown in the following list, the OOH provides information on required education and training, earnings, expected job prospects, nature of the work, and working conditions for hundreds of jobs. The OOH also gives you online search tips, links to job market information in all states, and other information such as advice on finding and applying for jobs.

Why are the five things listed important considerations? Knowing about the required amount of *training and education* for a certain job is important because if you lack the necessary education, you will not qualify for the job. If you want to be a lawyer, for example, but you do not plan to earn a bachelor's degree followed by a law degree, you may want to look into being a legal assistant or paralegal instead. Being aware of the training and education needed for different occupations will help you make a realistic choice.

Knowing what *earnings* are associated with different occupations is important to many workers. As discussed in chapter 3, different education levels are associated with different income levels and on average those with more education earn higher incomes. But there are differences within educational levels, and the OOH shows you expected earnings for specific jobs. For example, to be either an accountant or a K-12 teacher you need at least a bachelor's degree. But the median salary for accountants was $59,430 in 2008, whereas the median salary for teachers ranged from $47,100 to $51,180.

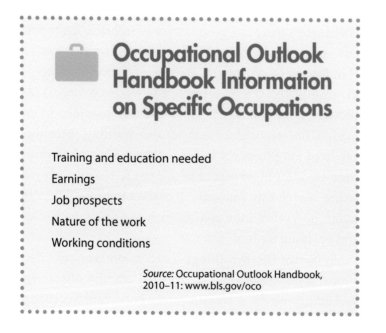

Occupational Outlook Handbook Information on Specific Occupations

Training and education needed

Earnings

Job prospects

Nature of the work

Working conditions

Source: Occupational Outlook Handbook, 2010–11: www.bls.gov/oco

The *job prospects* for each occupation on the OOH Web site tells you if there are expected to be more or fewer jobs in the occupation in the next 10 years. This is helpful in predicting if it will be easy or difficult to find a job. There is also information about how many people are employed in different occupations and where those positions are located. For example, there were about 642,000 people working as social workers in 2008. About 54 percent of social workers worked in health care or social assistance industries, and 31 percent worked for government agencies. Most social workers worked in cities or suburbs, but some worked in rural areas.

The OOH also provides valuable advice about job prospects within certain occupations. For example, as of 2008 the job prospects for social workers were reported to be favorable and social worker jobs were expected to grow faster than average in the next 10 years. This was especially true for social workers who worked with older adults or in rural areas. It may be more difficult to find employment as a social worker in cities that have colleges offering programs in social work because there may be more competition for those jobs.

If you think you would like to work in a certain type of job but would like to have more ideas about what those jobs entail, you can look at the *nature of the work* for occupations on the OOH Web site. For example, if you are interested in recreation but are not exactly sure what recreation workers might do, you would find that recreation workers plan, organize, and direct activities in a variety of places including playgrounds, parks, community and senior centers, and nursing homes. You would find that recreation workers lead group activities such as arts and crafts, sports, and performing arts. You would also find that recreation workers hold a variety of positions at different levels of responsibility.

Working conditions are described in the nature of the work and the *work environment* sections for the occupations of the OOH Web site. For example, you would find that the work environment for a forest or conservation worker is physically demanding. Forest workers work outdoors, sometimes in poor weather and in isolated areas. Jobs for forest workers are safer today than in the past due to the use of enclosed machines. You would find that the work environment of clinical laboratory technicians includes working with infectious specimens, but that few hazards exist since protective masks, gloves, and goggles are often used for safety reasons. You would further find that laboratories are usually well lighted and clean and that laboratory workers may spend a great deal of time on their feet. Knowing details about various occupations will help you to think about the type of job you would like to have.

LABOR MARKET FORCES AND JOB PROJECTIONS

If you have narrowed down your career choices, how do you know that there will be job openings available to you in your chosen occupation? How do you know that the job you get today will still exist in the future? No one can answer these questions with absolute certainty. But we can pin down several things that affect the likelihood that job openings will be available in the future. Job openings depend on many things including technology, the demand for goods and services, and the supply of workers.

Technology affects job openings because it affects the way goods and services are produced. For example, many people used to be employed to manually operate eleva-

OCCUPATIONS WITH THE FASTEST GROWTH

OCCUPATIONS	PERCENT CHANGE	NUMBER OF NEW JOBS (IN THOUSANDS)	WAGES (MAY 2008 MEDIAN)	EDUCATION/ TRAINING CATEGORY
Biomedical engineers	72	11.6	$ 77,400	Bachelor's degree
Network systems and data communications analyst	53	155.8	71,100	Bachelor's degree
Home health aides	50	460.9	20,460	Short-term on-the-job training
Personal and home care aides	46	375.8	19,180	Short-term on-the-job training
Financial examiners	41	11.1	70,930	Bachelor's degree
Medical scientists, except epidemiologists	40	44.2	72,590	Doctoral degree
Physician assistants	39	29.2	81,230	Master's degree
Skin care specialists	38	14.7	28,730	Postsecondary vocational award
Biochemists and biophysicists	37	8.7	82,840	Doctoral degree
Athletic trainers	37	6.0	39,640	Bachelor's degree
Physical therapist aides	36	16.7	23,760	Short-term on-the-job training
Dental hygienists	36	62.9	66,570	Associate degree
Veterinary technologists and technicians	36	28.5	28,900	Associate degree
Dental assistants	36	105.6	32,380	Moderate-term on-the-job training
Computer software engineers, applications	34	175.1	85,430	Bachelor's degree
Medical assistants	34	163.9	28,300	Moderate-term on-the-job training
Physical therapist assistants	33	21.2	46,140	Associate degree
Veterinarians	33	19.7	79,050	First professional degree
Self-enrichment education teachers	32	81.3	35,720	Work experience in a related occupation
Compliance officers, except agriculture, construction, health and safety, and transportation	31	80.8	48,890	Long-term on-the-job training

Source: BLS Occupational Employment Statistics and Division of Occupational Outlook

tors. After the invention of automatic elevators, this job became obsolete. Technological developments also lead to jobs in new industries such as the computer industry beginning in the 1980s, or in wind power. The demand for goods and services affects the jobs of people who produce those goods and services. If the demand for in-line skates falls, the demand for workers to produce in-line skates falls also. If demand for foreign travel increases, there will be more jobs in foreign travel fields.

Your likelihood of getting a certain job will depend on the supply of workers and how many other people qualify for it and want it. Related to this, competition from foreign workers can affect the number of job openings in certain occupations in the United States. If foreign workers are willing and able to work for lower salaries than U.S. workers, businesses may hire foreign workers for those jobs. Many more workers qualify for low-skilled jobs than for professional jobs, leading to higher unemployment among low-skilled workers.

The Bureau of Labor Statistics (BLS) provides an overview of 2008–18 job projections and factors affecting job openings and job prospects. They include the size of the population and the size of the labor force in their analysis. The *labor force* consists of those who are working or looking for work. The size of the labor force, and who is in it, changes when the population changes. The size of the U.S. population is expected to increase by about 11 percent from 2008–18, and the size of the labor force is expected to increase by about 8 percent during this period. The percentage of workers ages 55 and older is expected to increase more than any other age group, and the labor force is expected to become more diverse, with Blacks, Asians, and Hispanics increasing relative to Whites.

OCCUPATIONS WITH THE FASTEST DECLINE

OCCUPATIONS	PERCENT CHANGE	NUMBER OF LOST JOBS (IN THOUSANDS)	WAGES (MAY 2008 MEDIAN)	EDUCATION/ TRAINING CATEGORY
Textile bleaching and dyeing machine operators and tenders	−45	−7.2	$ 23,680	Moderate-term on-the-job training
Textile winding, twisting, and drawing out machine setters, operators, and tenders	−41	−14.2	23,970	Moderate-term on-the-job training
Textile knitting and weaving machine setters, operators, and tenders	−39	−11.5	25,400	Long-term on-the-job
Shoe machine operators and tenders	−35	−1.7	25,090	Moderate-term on-the-job training
Extruding and forming machine setters, operators, and tenders, synthetic and glass fibers	−34	−4.8	31,160	Moderate-term on-the-job training
Sewing machine operators	−34	−71.5	19,870	Moderate-term on-the-job training
Semiconductor processors	−32	−10.0	32,230	Postsecondary vocational award
Textile cutting machine setters, operators, and tenders	−31	−6.0	22,620	Moderate-term on-the-job training
Postal Service mail sorters, processors, and processing machine operators	−30	−54.5	50,020	Short-term on-the-job
Fabric menders, except garment	−30	−0.3	28,470	Moderate-term on-the-job training
Wellhead pumpers	−28	−5.3	37,860	Moderate-term on-the-job training
Fabric and apparel patternmakers	−27	−2.2	37,760	Long-term on-the-job-training

OCCUPATIONS WITH THE FASTEST DECLINE (CON'T)

OCCUPATIONS	PERCENT CHANGE	NUMBER OF LOST JOBS (IN THOUSANDS)	WAGES (MAY 2008 MEDIAN)	EDUCATION/ TRAINING CATEGORY
Drilling and boring machine tool setters, operators, and tenders, metal and plastic	–27	–8.9	30,850	Moderate-term on-the-job training
Lathe and turning machine tool setters, operators, and tenders, metal and plastic	–27	–14.9	32,940	Moderate-term on-the-job training
Order clerks	–26	–64.2	27,990	Short-term on-the-job training
Coil winders, tapers, and finishers	–25	–5.6	27,730	Short-term on-the-job-training
Photographic processing machine	–24	–12.5	20,360	Short-term on-the-job-training
File clerks	–23	–49.6	23,800	Short-term on-the-job-training
Derrick operators, oil and gas	–23	–5.8	41,920	Moderate-term on-the-job training
Desktop publishers	–23	–5.9	36,600	Postsecondary vocational award

Source: BLS Occupational Employment Statistics and Division of Occupational Outlook

The BLS predicts that total employment will increase by 10 percent by 2018, but the increases will be greater in some areas than others. This is due in part to changes in technology and demand for goods and services. Employment in industries that produce goods has decreased in the United States since the 1990s, and manufacturing jobs are expected to continue to fall. Jobs in the United States are shifting from the production of goods to the production of services. It is expected that many new jobs will exist in the future in the service fields of health care, social assistance, professional and scientific services, educational services, and other services.

The table on page 91 lists the 20 occupations that are expected to have the fastest growth between 2008 and 2018, along with wages and education needed for the jobs. Note that nine of these occupations require a bachelor's degree or higher and three require an associate degree. The table on page 93 lists occupations with the fastest expected decline. Note that none of these occupations requires an associate degree or higher. It is clear that having a job requiring a college degree makes it less likely that the job will cease to exist in the future. Low-skilled jobs are much more likely to become obsolete.

FINDING A JOB

How can you find that perfect job? If you have decided what occupations you are interested in and qualified for, your next step is locating jobs to which you would like to apply. There are many places where you can look to find job openings. The sidebar provides a list of places to learn about job openings, as reported by the BLS. Many people find jobs through friends, family, neighbors, teachers, and other acquaintances, so your *personal contacts* can be a good source of information about job openings. Be sure to let people know that you are looking for a job, and consider joining new organizations to increase your contacts. Your *high school or college placement office* probably has job counseling services and lists of job openings. They may be able to help you write résumés and cover letters and prepare for interviews as well.

Many successful job seekers contact *employers* directly to locate job openings. Find out what companies employ people in your chosen occupation, and then frequently check their Web sites for job openings. You may wish to contact potential employers about your interest in working for them even if no job openings are currently

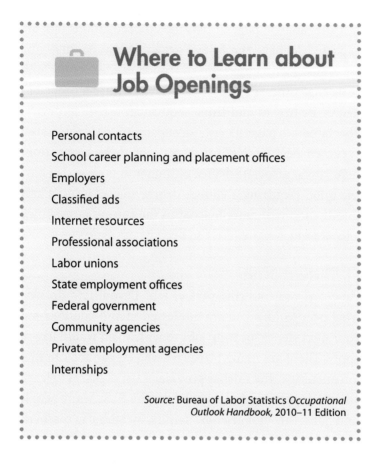

Where to Learn about Job Openings

Personal contacts

School career planning and placement offices

Employers

Classified ads

Internet resources

Professional associations

Labor unions

State employment offices

Federal government

Community agencies

Private employment agencies

Internships

Source: Bureau of Labor Statistics *Occupational Outlook Handbook,* 2010–11 Edition

posted. You can also ask for an informational interview with someone in the career in which you are interested. People may remember you and recommend you when an opening becomes available.

There are several sources of *classified ads* that list available jobs. These include newspapers, professional journals, and trade magazines. Professional journals and trade magazines are publications associated with specific careers, such as nursing, electronics, and public safety. Because jobs may fill quickly, you should respond to classified ads promptly. There are also many *resources on the Internet* designed to help those with jobs to fill and those seeking jobs. There are both national and local Web sites, and some are related to jobs in specific fields. You can also search the Internet for professional associations that may post jobs in their field. Keep in mind that some Web sites may not be current or may only provide links to other Web sites where jobs have been posted directly.

If you search the Internet for a *professional association* in a career field, you may discover that the association has job placement services and job advice for job seekers in that profession. For example, the American Economic Association offers career advice to future economists and organizes a job market for those seeking postsecondary teaching and research positions in economics. Frequently you must join the association to take advantage of their services. *Labor unions* also offer job services and may have apprentice programs where you can learn a skill while you work. Contact the appropriate labor union or visit their Web site for more information.

Every state has a *State Employment Service* office and a list of online resources to help you find jobs in the state. These offices are listed at www.job-hunt.org. These offices offer employment counseling to help you discover your interests and abilities and to prepare for careers. If you are interested in working for the federal government, you should contact USAJOBS, the federal government's official source for job and employment information (www.usajobs.gov). You can search for jobs by keyword and by location at USAJOBS.

Nonprofit *community agencies* such as religious or vocational rehabilitation organizations often offer employment services to target groups such as women, minorities, or young people. There are also *private employment agencies* and consultants who offer these services, but be aware that they may charge fees, such as a percentage of your first year's salary. The fee may be paid by the you, the job seeker, or by the employer. Given that there are many services available that do not charge fees, make sure that the benefits of these organizations are worth the costs.

Consider taking an *internship* at a business, as this may lead to an offer of permanent employment. An *internship* is a type of work experience where you have supervised practical training for a certain job. The pay is usually less than for a regular position and internships are offered for a limited time period, such as six months. However internships are a way to get job experience and training. You may also consider volunteering for a business where you would like to work. When the employer gets to know you, this may result in a permanent offer when a job comes available.

APPLYING FOR A JOB

Did you find a job opening that interests you? Now it is time to make the formal application. Many jobs require that you fill out an application form and also submit a résumé and cover letter. If the employer is interested in you, you may be invited to an interview so you can meet each other in person. Let us look into these topics now.

The Job Application Form

Depending on the position and employer to which you are applying, application forms may be available online, by mail, or you may pick them up in person. What information will you need to provide on a job application? Application forms will generally ask you for contact information including your name, mailing address, e-mail address, and phone number. You will be asked what job or what type of job you are seeking, and about your skills and experience. You will be asked questions about your education, including what schools you have attended, what degrees you have received and when, and in what subjects you specialized. You will be asked about your work experience. If you have worked before, be prepared to list job titles, name and contact information for employers, and the dates when you worked for each job. You can also include volunteer work. You may be asked to describe your job duties and the reason for leaving prior jobs. You may also be asked to supply names and contact information of references. Your references should be people who know you and who can talk about your abilities, such as teachers, coaches, or former employers. Be sure to ask people in advance for permission to list them as a reference.

When you fill out the job application, try to make your answers address the qualities mentioned in the announcement of the job opening. For example, if the job announcement says that they are looking for someone with good skills in word processing and spreadsheet programs, be sure to list any skills that you have with those programs. Where possible, tailor your answers on the application to the specific job to which you are applying.

Make sure that your application is neat, accurate, and complete. Check carefully to make sure that there are no spelling or punctuation errors. Your application is part of your first introduction to your potential employer, and you want to be sure to make a good impression.

The Résumé

A résumé is a short document that provides an easy-to-view summary of information about you. Much of the information on your résumé will be the same as that on your job application form. Your résumé will contain information about your education, job history, and other experiences that pertain to the particular job to which you are applying. Your résumé provides an opportunity to show your strengths. You may be able to tailor your résumé to emphasize how your skills and experience meet the requirements of a specific job.

Your résumé should be short and concise, using bullet points rather than sentences and paragraphs. There are many different formats for résumés and there are many sample résumés available on the Internet. Before you decide on a format and what you want to include in your résumé, you should look at many sample résumés. The figure provides an example of a template for a résumé. Although formats may differ, your name and contact information should appear at the top. There are usually headers identifying the different sections of the résumé. It should be accurate, neat, free of errors, and easy to read.

There are several sections that should be included in any résumé. These include your job objective, your work experience, your education, and contact information. The following sample also includes sections for your accomplishments and professional skills. You might also wish to include sections on community service. Your job objective can be tailored to the specific position to which you are applying. The section on work experience is usually broken down by the company you worked for and the position you held. If you are applying for your first job, you can list work such as babysitting, volunteer work, or community service. The school you have last attended and the highest degree you earned should be listed first in the education section. If your grade point average is

SAMPLE RÉSUMÉ TEMPLATE

NAME
street address
city, state, zip code
phone number
email address

OBJECTIVE
What do you want to do in the jobs for which you are applying?

EDUCATION
• List your highest degree, name of school, date earned
• List other degrees earned or educational programs completed, names of school, dates earned

ACCOMPLISHMENTS
• If relevant, list any academic awards you have earned
• If relevant, list any other special things that you have done or achieved

WORK EXPERIENCE
• List names of places and locations of places where you have worked, positions held, and dates worked

PROFESSIONAL SKILLS
List any special skills that you have that are relevant to the workplace such as
• foreign language proficiency
• proficiency with computer programs
• skills you have gained in prior jobs
• other relevant job related skills and experiences

REFERENCES
• You may say that references are provided on request
• Or you may provide names and contact information of people who have agreed to serve as your references

impressive, you could include that information. In the reference section, it is common to say that references will be provided upon request, especially if you are asked to provide references in your job application.

The Cover Letter

Many employers ask you to submit a cover letter along with your résumé and the job application form. Some career counselors suggest that you always include a cover letter when you submit a résumé to apply for a job. The cover letter helps to introduce you to the potential employer. Write your cover letter in a standard business letter format. A cover letter allows you to provide more in-depth information than is included in your résumé and lets you explain why you are applying for a specific job. Cover letters are usually one page and may consist of three short paragraphs.

Following a business letter format, your cover letter will include your address and the name and address of the person to whom your letter is addressed at the top of the page. You should state what position you are applying for and why you are interested in the company and the position. You should state your main qualifications for the position. Most cover letters request an interview or mention that you would like to arrange an interview. You should include a phone number where you may be reached and also an e-mail address. A sample cover based on an Industry Canada letter is shown here. As with résumés, there are many sample cover letters available on the Internet that you may look at before writing your own.

The Job Interview

If you are asked invited to a job interview, it means that the employer has viewed your application (and résumé and cover letter) favorably and would like to get to know you better. A job interview is a chance to show your personality, your enthusiasm, and your strengths. There are several ways that you can prepare for an interview to help you present yourself in the best way. The following sug-

SAMPLE COVER LETTER

Applicant's Name
Address
Phone Number
email address

Company Name
Name of the person in charge of hiring
Title
Address

Date

Dear Mr. or Ms. (Name of the person who is in charge of hiring).
Or Sir/Madam:

With reference to your advertisement in the Local News on August 28, I wish to apply for the position of clerk at your video store.

I believe I have the necessary skills and abilities for this job. I am organized, resourceful, personable, and a fast learner. I am also fluent in both official languages.

Your company excels at customer service, a field in which I would like to pursue a career. I am also very eager to become part of a winning team such as yours. Joining your organization would give me the chance to develop useful skills that will help in pursuing my long-term career goals.

If you are interested in meeting with me, I am available for an interview weekdays after 3:30 P.M. or at any time on the weekend.

I look forward to hearing from you.

Signature

Encl. (résumé)

Source: Industry Canada

gestions follow those from the *BLS Occupational Outlook Handbook*, 2010–11 and from an article "Big Blunders Job Hunters Make" from the *Wall Street Journal* (6/28/2010).

Interviewees are advised to dress appropriately and be prepared to discuss their qualifications. *(Shutterstock)*

Preparation: Learn about the organization before you go to the interview. This shows that you are interested in the business. Be prepared to discuss your qualifications for a specific job or jobs, and to describe your experience. Be aware that you might be asked broad questions such as "Why do you want this job?" of "What are your strengths and weaknesses?" Ask someone to help you practice for the interview.

Personal Appearance: Make sure that you are clean and neat. Do not smoke or chew gum. Dress appropriately for the position. For example, if you are applying to work in an office and everyone wears a suit and tie, you should wear this to the interview. If you are applying to work as a teacher's aide in a school, dress the way the teachers dress. When in doubt, dress more formally as opposed to more casually.

The Interview: Plan to arrive a little early. Do not bring friends or family with you. Turn off your cell phone. Learn the name of the person interviewing you and say hello with a firm handshake, using eye contact. Do not begin by asking about pay and benefits. Use good manners and do not use slang. Relax, but do not slouch. Show that you are cooperative and enthusiastic. Concisely answer each question you are asked. Ask questions about the organization and job, but do not ask questions that you could easily answer from reading the company Web site. When the interview is over, shake hands with the interviewer. Send a short thank you note to the interviewer promptly.

Things to Bring: You should bring your social security card, driver's license or government-issued identification, a copy of your résumé and application, a list of three references, and copies of your school transcripts. You may not be asked to show all of these things, but the employer may wish to see them if they are considering offering you a job.

SUMMARY

Choosing a career and looking for a job can be both fun and exciting. Thinking about your interests, abilities, and values is a good way to get started, and there are many resources available to help you do this. Whether you are applying for your first job or are looking for a job change, whether you are looking for a job after finishing school or a part-time job while in college, finding a job you enjoy can be very rewarding. Even if you are not entering the job market at this time, knowing how to locate job openings, how to apply for jobs, how to write a résumé and cover letter, and what to expect in a job interview are all valuable skills for the future. Fortunately there are many reputable sources available to help you in choosing your career and finding the right job, as these are among the most important decisions you will make in your life.

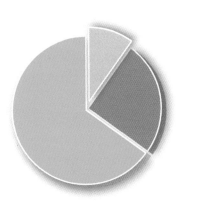

6

On the Job

Congratulations! You have found a job, or you are well on your way to finding a job. This may be a part-time job or a full-time job. It may be a job that you plan to keep while you finish school, or it may be a job that you hope to keep for the rest of your life. Whatever the situation, there is certain information about being employed that is relevant for you. How can you make sense of your paycheck? What can you do to try to make sure that you are successful in your job and to avoid getting fired? What rules and laws are important in the workplace? These are some of the questions that are answered in this chapter.

UNDERSTANDING YOUR PAYCHECK

You know how much money you are making on your job, so why doesn't your paycheck not seem to add up to your wages or salary? Let us say that in your first job after you graduate from college, you are earning $4,000 per month working for the ABC Corporation. You are paid once a month. When you receive your first paycheck, you expect to see $4,000.00. Why is the check for significantly less than the $4,000 you expected?

Understanding your paycheck involves understanding the various deductions that are made from your gross pay. *Gross pay* is the total amount you earn in a pay period before any deductions such as taxes are taken out of your paycheck. *Net pay* is the amount you receive after deductions are taken out. Your net pay is the actual amount of the check, and it is frequently only about 65–70 percent of the gross amount. Your net pay is what you have to spend.

Common Paycheck Deductions

When you get paid, you may receive a check attached to a pay stub. The *pay stub* will show the deductions that were made from your check. The figure at right shows a sample pay stub. Different places of employment have different pay stub designs and include different types of information, so your pay stub will not look exactly like this. If you arrange to have your paycheck automatically deposited into your bank account, your pay stub will probably indicate this. To understand some of the most common paycheck deductions, let us look at the sample pay stub shown below.

Your place of employment, in this case the ABC Corporation, is written on the pay stub. Your name and social security number (SSN) are shown. Your gross pay is $4,000.00 for the month of March 2011. However, the actual amount of the check is $2,749.00. This is your net pay, which is also called your take-home pay. Economists sometimes use the term disposable income for net pay. *Disposable income* refers to the income that is available to you for spending or saving, after taxes have been paid. The

SAMPLE PAY STUB

ABC Corporation

Employee: **Gross Earnings: $4000.00**

Your Name
SSN: 000-00-0000
Pay Period: 3/1/11–3/31/11

Deductions:

Federal Income Tax	$ 600.00
State Income Tax	$ 160.00
Social Security (FICA)	$ 248.00
Medicare (FICA)	$ 58.00
Retirement Savings Plan	$ 100.00
Medical Insurance	$ 85.00
	$1,251.00

Net Pay: **$2,749.00**

---

deductions shown on the sample pay stub total $1,251.00. *Deductions* in this case represent the amount subtracted from your gross pay to give you your net pay. The sample shows six deductions:

Federal Income Tax: Most workers are required to pay taxes on their income to the federal government. The amount that you pay depends on how much you earn. It is computed as a percentage of your income. The higher your income, the higher the percentage that you pay, ranging up to 35 percent for those earning more than $373,650 in 2010. On the sample pay stub, the federal income tax deduction is $600. This is 15 percent of your total income of $4,000. The money that the federal government receives in taxes is used to finance federal government spending on programs such as the military, highways, national parks, and education.

The amount of income tax deducted from your paycheck is a type of *withholding tax*. This means that the money is deducted from your paycheck in advance of the taxes being due. Your total federal income taxes are not due until April 15 each year, when you file a tax return. If the amount of withholding is greater than the total amount you owe, you will receive a refund. If the amount of withholding is less that the amount you owe, you will have to make an additional payment.

Employers know how much tax to withhold from your paycheck based on the W-4 form that you fill out when you are hired. The *W-4* is a federal form that the Internal Revenue Service (IRS) requires. How you fill in the information at the top of the W-4 form affects how much is withheld from your paycheck. The more exemptions you list in lines A through G, the less your employer will withhold from your paycheck for federal income taxes.

State Income Tax: State income tax is another deduction shown on the sample pay stub. In most states, workers are required to pay state income taxes in addition to federal income taxes. The amount that you pay varies from state to state. The sample pay stub shows that $160 was withheld from your paycheck for state income taxes.

Social Security (FICA):   FICA refers to the Federal Insurance Contributions Act. *FICA* is a payroll tax (sometimes called an employment tax) used to provide funds for both the Social Security program and the Medicare program. The *Social Security* program was introduced by the federal government in the 1930s to provide benefits for retired people, disabled people, and children of deceased workers. Most wage-earners pay FICA taxes. In 2010, workers contributed 6.2 percent of their gross income to

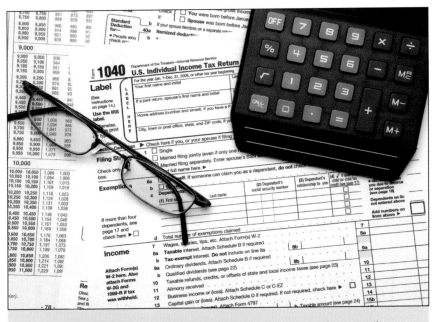

According to the Internal Revenue Service, more than 2 million tax returns were filed by people below the age of 18. (*Shutterstock*)

Social Security, up to an income limit of $106,800. The deduction for the contribution to Social Security shown in the sample is $248.00, or 6.2 percent of $4,000.

Employers also make FICA contributions for their workers. In 2010, the employer's contribution to Social Security was also 6.2 percent of the worker's gross income. When you retire, the amount of Social Security retirement income that you receive is based on how long you worked and your earned income, but you do not necessarily receive the exact amount of your contributions.

The Social Security tax is an example of a regressive tax. A *regressive tax* is one where lower income people pay a higher percentage of their income in taxes. Since no

Social Security taxes are paid on incomes over $106,800, those with incomes above this level end up paying a lower percentage in taxes than those with lower incomes. For example, someone whose income was exactly $106,800 would pay 6.2 percent or $6,621.60 in Social Security taxes in 2010. The maximum amount that any worker paid in 2010 is $6,621.60. So someone whose income was $200,000 would also pay $6,621.60. This would be 3.3 percent of their total income of $200,000. Because the higher income worker pays a lower percentage of income in Social Security taxes, the tax is regressive.

Medicare: The next deduction shown on the sample pay stub is for Medicare. Another program supported by FICA taxes, *Medicare* provides hospital insurance benefits for people aged 65 or older. Some other people may also receive benefits from Medicare, including some disabled people and people with certain qualifying diseases. In 2010, both workers and employers contributed 1.45 percent of the worker's gross pay to Medicare. Therefore, if your gross pay was $4,000, your contribution would be $58.00, as shown in the sample.

Retirement Savings Plan: Some companies have plans to help you to save for retirement so you will have money in addition to your Social Security income. Your company may have a plan where this can be deducted from your paycheck. A common example of this type of a retirement plan is a 401(k). With a *401(k),* you decide how much you want to contribute toward your retirement and your employer puts the money into an account for you. Your employer's plan would have a selection of investments from which you could choose. Sometimes employers also contribute money to your plan when you decide to contribute. The sample pay stub shows that you are contributing $100 to your retirement plan. The ABC Corporation may have a matching plan where, for example, they would contribute 50 percent of what you contribute. In this case, they would put $50 in your retirement account for every $100 that you contribute.

Medical Insurance: Businesses sometimes provide some form of medical insurance for their employees. Medical insurance is also called health insurance. Sometimes the business does not pay the full 100 percent of the cost of medical insurance, so the employee pays part of it. The part that you pay would be a deduction from your paycheck. In the sample, you are paying $85 a month toward your medical insurance and the ABC Corporation is paying the rest. Having medical insurance can greatly reduce the cost of health care if you are sick or injured.

The Bottom Line

The sample pay stub shows that although your gross pay is $4,000, your net pay is $2,749.00. The net pay is $4,000 minus the total of all the deductions. If you add up the deductions shown ($600 + $160 + $248 + $58 + $100 + $85) you get a total of $1,251. Subtracting the total deductions from $4,000 gives you $2,749.00. This is the actual amount of your paycheck and the amount that you have available to spend. When planning a budget, it is important to realize that your net pay may only be 65–70 percent of your gross pay. If you make spending plans thinking that you would have $4,000 rather than $2,749, you could be in trouble.

It is also important to know that the sample pay stub is only an example. You need to become familiar with your own pay stub to see exactly what the situation is for you.

KEEPING YOUR JOB AND MOVING UP

There are many advantages to having a job that you like. If you are working full-time, you are spending many of your waking hours at work. If you are happy in your job and know that you are appreciated, this can be important for your satisfaction with your life in general. Getting fired from a job that you like could be your worst nightmare. Not only do you lose your income, you also lose the satisfaction that comes from knowing that you are a valued member of the workforce and able to earn your own money.

Sometimes getting fired or laid off is out of your control. For example, the economy could be in a recession, forcing many businesses to have to lay off employees. A *recession* occurs when overall output declines in the economy. If not as much is produced, businesses do not need as many workers, causing some people to lose their jobs. When the economy recovers and overall output begins to increase again, there would be more jobs available again. There are other times, however, when keeping your job can be within your control.

Strategies for Being Successful at Work (and to Avoid Being Fired)

There are some things that you can do that will likely help you to be successful in your job and to avoid being fired from your job. These strategies involve how you act in your place of work and how you interact with others. We will look at some of these strategies now:[2]

---

[2]Some of the strategies discussed in this section are based on a 2006 article by Mary Nemko entitled "How to Avoid Being Fired" (Kiplinger) and a 2007 article by Joseph Baylon entitled "Top 10 Ways to Avoid Getting Fired" (Associated Content from Yahoo.)

Strategies to Avoid Being Fired from Your Job

Be on time

Be loyal

Be honest

Be polite and respectful

Avoid unnecessary absences

Be positive

Watch your behavior at all times

Learn and understand your company's priorities

Form solid working relationships

Learn how your boss wants you to work

Be a hard worker

Get feedback on how you are doing

- *Be on time.* Being late is a common reason for being fired. If you are cutting it so close that you are late for work when your bus is a little late, then take an earlier bus. Being on time includes not just arriving for work on time, but also being on time for meetings, appointments, and other workplace commitments. Being on time shows respect for your colleagues because if you are late for a meeting, you are wasting your colleague's time as they wait for you.

- *Be loyal.* Being loyal means that your actions show that you are committed to your job and to your company. You demonstrate loyalty by speaking well of your company and your boss, by doing your best work, and by being cooperative. Be loyal to your coworkers also. Do not gossip to or about your coworkers and be a team player.

- *Be honest.* Even very minor amounts of employee fraud are serious. If you work in an office, do not take workplace supplies home. Do not use the office computer for your personal business. If you work in a restaurant, do not eat the restaurant food without permission. Know the rules that pertain to where you work and follow them. Be honest about when you arrive and when you leave and how long your breaks are.

- *Be polite and respectful.* If you are rude to your boss, your boss will likely not want to keep you on your job, even if you are good at it. Do not argue with your boss. Always be polite and respectful to your coworkers also. Making an effort to get along with everyone can have big payoffs. Everyone is happier and able to accomplish more in a friendly environment where people practice mutual respect.

- *Avoid unnecessary absences.* Carefully follow your company's policies about sick leave and vacation leave. Being absent can make things harder for you and for your coworkers. If your boss finds that he or she can get along without you, he or she may decide to do just that.

- *Be positive.* Being happy, cheerful, and optimistic spreads good will and reflects well on you. If your job involves working with customers, this is especially important.

- *Watch your behavior at all times.* It goes without saying that you have to act appropriately at the workplace. But if you get in trouble outside of work, this can hurt your overall reputation. Also watch your behavior at social functions associated with work such as holiday parties. Be careful about what you post on social network sites.

- *Learn and understand your company's priorities.* Get the important things done first. Pay careful attention to what your boss tells you about what you should be doing and when.

- *Form solid working relationships.* Be a team player. Be a trusted coworker. It is usually much harder for a boss to fire someone he or she likes than someone who is not well-liked.

- *Learn how your boss wants you to work.* Does he or she want to know what you are doing at all times? Or would he or she prefer that you work very independently? Does your boss prefer to communicate with you in person, by phone, or by e-mail? Find out your boss's preferences and then follow them.

- *Be a hard worker.* Don't act bored or act like you are anxious to go home. Productive workers are valuable to the business.

- *Get feedback on how you are doing.* Listen when people tell you what they do or do not like about your work. Many workplaces have regular schedules for letting workers know how they are doing. If your boss gives you suggestions for improvement, try to follow through.

So You Think You Deserve a Promotion or a Raise?[3]

If you get a *raise,* this means that you earn a higher salary and are paid more money for doing your job. Often, getting a raise is associated with getting a promotion. If you get a *promotion,* you are assigned to a higher-level position with more responsibilities. Some jobs have standardized steps for promotions and raises. For example, for many public school teachers, an additional year of experience leads to an automatic salary increase. This is also true in some government jobs. Some private companies also have standard procedures for evaluating employees for promotion and salary increases. In other circumstances, the process for moving up the career ladder is not as clear. You need to be aware of the process for your own situation. Keep in mind that a promotion may bring with it higher pay, but it will also bring more responsibilities and may require harder work.

---

[3]Some of the recommendations in this section are based on the following. Maria Hanson, "9 Tips for Getting a Promotion." LiveCareer. Available online. URL: http://www.livecareer.com/news/Career/9-Tips-for-Getting-a-Promotion $$01381.aspx. Accessed June 1, 2011; Yahoo! HotJobs 2010; and Randall Hansen, "Moving Up the Ladder: 10 Strategies for Getting Yourself Promoted." Quintessential Careers 2010. Available online. URL: http://www.quintcareers.com/getting promoted strategies.html. Accessed June 1, 2011.

Planning for a promotion: If you are interested in advancing, you should have a plan to show your company that you deserve and can handle the additional responsibility. Think ahead. What job would you like to have, and what would you have to do to be good at that job? Do you need to have additional training? Do you need to take classes or attend workshops to learn new skills? Do what it takes to prepare yourself for the job you want. While you are preparing, show that you are a hard worker who deserves to get ahead. Show interest in the company. Offer positive suggestions that may help the business succeed. Show that you are a leader and that you are interested in the future of your company.

To prepare yourself to move up to a more responsible job, work to build relationships with people in the level of job that you are seeking. If you have a mentor who is in a higher position, he or she may provide you with insights and information. He or she can also help to let others know about your skills and ambitions. Work to expand your network of contacts in your place of work. Your *network* is the group of people with whom you are connected. If more people know about your strong points, there is a greater chance that someone will remember you and recommend you for a position that becomes open.

To show your superiors that you are ready to advance, consider asking for increased responsibilities, and then show that you can handle these new tasks. Be willing and available to learn new jobs. The more you know how to do, the more value you have to your company. Learning new jobs and knowing a variety of jobs can also put you in a position to move to a new department in the company.

Asking for a promotion or raise: Sometimes a boss may offer a promotion and raise to a worthy employee. But in other circumstances it may be appropriate for you to bring up the topic with your boss or whoever is in charge of promotions and raises. Find out what procedures are appropriate in your organization. Several commonsense strategies apply if you decide to ask your boss for a promotion or a salary increase.

Be able to justify your request. Consider writing down a list of your accomplishments to discuss with your boss. Exactly what have you accomplished? What have you done in your current job that shows that you deserve more pay? What are your significant contributions at the workplace? Have you taken on increased responsibilities? Thinking about the answers to questions like these will prepare you to give good reasons for why you think you deserve to be promoted and to earn more money.

If you have a meeting with your boss to discuss your request for a raise or promotion, be polite and respectful. You can discuss your achievements without bragging and without sounding conceited. Do not compare yourself to your fellow workers in a way that makes them look bad. You may be asked how much of a raise you think you deserve. Find out beforehand how much typical raises are in your company and for people at your level. Do not make an unreasonable request.

If your boss tells you no, you cannot have that promotion or raise, listen carefully to the reasons why your request is being turned down. Is it because of a downturn in the economy in general? Is it because your boss does not think that you stand out compared to your coworkers? Find out what you can do to improve so that the next time around, the response will be more likely to be yes.

WORKPLACE RULES AND LAWS

As a worker, you have the right to be treated fairly. Although your legal rights vary depending on things such as whether you are a part-time worker or a full-time worker, all workers are protected by certain laws. The U.S. Department of Labor (DOL) provides information to American workers, employers, job seekers, and retired workers about federal employment laws. The DOL is committed to protecting the "wages, health benefits, retirement security, employment rights, safety, and health of America's workforce." (www.dol.gov/compliance/). We will now look at some of your rights as a worker as outlined by the U.S. Department of Labor.

Wages and Hours Worked

There are several laws that affect the wages and work hours of workers. The Fair Labor Standards Act (FLSA) requires payment of no less than the federal minimum wage for covered workers, and also provides for payment of overtime pay for working more than 40 hours per week. In 2010, the federal minimum wage was $7.25 per hour. However, some categories of workers can legally be paid less than the minimum wage, including some student workers. There is a different minimum wage for people under 20 years old for the first 90 days that they work. As of 2010, this wage was $4.25 per hour.

The FLSA does not specify a maximum number of hours per day or days per week that a worker age 16 or older can work. Some states do have laws that limit the maximum hours of work per week, however. The FLSA also does not regulate issues related to vacation pay, sick pay, or pay raises.

Benefits: Health, Retirement, and Leave

The DOL oversees several laws and regulations regarding employment benefits. The Employment Retirement Income Security Act (ERISA) pertains to retirement benefits and health plans. Most pension plans and group health plans conducted by private sector businesses are covered by ERISA. *Private sector* refers to that part of the economy that is not controlled by the government. These laws ensure that members of the retirement plans and health plans have access to information about them and that those who manage the plans meet certain standards of conduct. Federal laws do not require businesses to provide retirement or health benefits for all employees.

A worker's right to take a leave of absence from a job for the birth of a child, for his or her own health problems, or to care for a member of the immediate family is governed by the Family and Medical Leave Act (FMLA.) This act says that you are entitled to up to 12 weeks of unpaid leave during any 12 month period for these reasons. The FMLA also ensures that you would not lose your group health benefits during the leave. However, many factors pertaining to leaves are matters of agreement between an employer and an employee. For example, the Federal Labor Standards Act does not require an employer to pay you for time not worked while on vacation, attending a funeral, or on jury duty. The FLSA also does not require an employer to give you a certain number of paid sick days.

Hiring and Termination Issues

Employers must follow federal laws when they hire workers. Some of these laws make it illegal to discriminate in hiring decisions due to race, color, ethnicity, religion, sex, age, national origin, disability, or veteran status. Equal employment opportunity (EEO) laws prohibit specific types of employment discrimination in both hiring and terminating workers. The DOL also oversees laws pertaining to workers under age 18, veterans, and some foreign workers.

When terminating or leaving a job, some workers have rights to continue group health insurance plans for a limited time. And some workers qualify to receive unemployment insurance benefits. The federal unemployment insurance program provides wages for people who become unemployed for reasons that are not their fault (as defined by state laws). Under this program, unemployment benefits are provided to workers who meet specified eligibility requirements such as having worked for a certain length of time. If you get fired for cause or quit a job, you will likely not qualify for unemployment benefits.

Equal Opportunity

It is illegal to discriminate against workers in hiring and termination decisions, and it is also illegal to discriminate against workers in many areas on the job for reasons based on race, religion, sex, or national origin. For example, discrimination is not allowed in areas that affect pay rates, promotions, layoffs, and selection for training programs. Sexual harassment is considered to be discrimination based on sex. Laws against this type of discrimination fall into the category of Equal Employment Opportunity (EEO) laws, like laws against discrimination in hiring and terminating workers.

Safety and Health in the Workplace

Many of the laws that cover safety and health in the workplace are administered by the DOL's Occupational Safety

Though child labor standards vary by state, the Fair Labor Standards Act (FLSA) stipulates that a minor below the age of 16 may work a maximum of 40 hours a week during a nonschool-day period. *(Shutterstock)*

and Health Administration (OSHA.) Most workers in the United States are protected by OSHA or OSHA-approved plans. Under the Occupational Safety and Health Act, employers are obligated to provide work and a place of work that are "free from recognized, serious hazards." Rules affecting workers under age 18 are covered by the Fair Labor Standards Act.

Whistle-blower Protection

A *whistle-blower* is someone who reports that something is wrong in the workplace and hopes that reporting the wrongdoing will help to stop it. A number of laws make it illegal for someone to act against you because you complained about unsafe or unhealthy working conditions, environmental problems, and some other activities. The Occupational Safety and Health Act (OSH Act) is one of the laws that protects workers from being transferred, denied a raise, having their work hours reduced, and being fired or otherwise punished because they reported unsafe or unhealthy working conditions.

Labor Unions

Under the National Labor Relations Act of 1935, workers have the right to join a labor union or to help to organize a labor union if there is not one available. A *labor union* is as an organization of employees formed to bargain with the employer. Union members believe that their chances of receiving better pay and working conditions are greater through collective bargaining than if each worker negotiated with the employer by himself or herself. *Collective bargaining* occurs when a union negotiates with an employer for all the workers who are associated with the union. It is against the law for employers to punish workers who participate in union activities. Workers have the right to bargain collectively for higher pay, increased benefits, better working conditions, and more favorable rules affecting their jobs. Workers have the right to select their own union representatives who will bargain for them. If workers want to form a labor union, the National Labor Relations Board (NLRB) is the federal agency that holds elections to see if a majority of the employees are in favor of forming a labor union.

Sometimes workers may be required to join a union. This is called a *union shop.* Union shops are prohibited in states that have right-to-work laws. In a state with *right-to-work* laws, workers cannot be forced to join a union in order to keep their jobs. *Closed shops,* where only union members can be hired, are also illegal in states that have right-to-work laws.

SUMMARY

In this chapter, we have discussed some of the important things associated with the workplace, including understanding your paycheck, strategies for keeping your job, and strategies for moving up. We have also discussed some, but by no means all, of the rules, laws, and regulations applying to the workplace. It is important to recognize that in addition to federal laws, states and other localities such as counties and cities may have other laws that affect the rights of both workers and employers. These laws cannot conflict with or negate the federal laws, but they may add additional rules and rights. For example, as mentioned earlier, different states have different rules and requirements about overtime hours and work hours. And different states have different rules about joining labor unions. As well, different places of employment have their own rules. As a worker, it is important for you to know the rules and regulations that apply to you in your job so that workplace rules and laws can protect you.

Test Your Knowledge

1. Education obtained after high school is called:
   a. elementary education
   b. secondary education
   c. postsecondary or higher education
   d. high school education

2. When someone receives a bachelor's degree from a four-year college or university, she/he is called a
   a. vocational school graduate
   b. Ph.D.
   c. community-college graduate
   d. college graduate

3. In the United States, the role of the federal government in education
   a. is limited by the Constitution. State and local governments have more control.
   b. is extensive. Most decisions about education are made at the federal level.
   c. consists of overseeing the day-to-day operation of schools, including hiring and licensing teachers.
   d. is non-existent. The federal government has nothing to do with education.

4. Say that you are choosing between going to a four-year college or working for four years at a local grocery store. The *opportunity cost* of going to college is

    a. the tuition, fees, and other outlays that you would spend to attend the college

    b. the income, benefits, training, and experience you would acquire if you worked at the grocery store

    c. the dollars spent on going to a four-year college minus the dollars you would have spent had you attended a two-year college

    d. the amount of income you will make as a college graduate plus what you would make as a high-school graduate

5. Say that you are considering applying to private colleges, public colleges, in-state colleges, and out-of-state colleges. Which of the following choices is *usually* less expensive in terms of stated charges for tuition and fees?

    a. a public in-state school

    b. a private out-of-state school

    c. a public out-of-state school

    d. a private in-state school

6. Which of the following statements is true with respect to financial aid for higher education?

    a. financial aid is only available for students with financial need

    b. financial aid is only available for students with straight-A grade point averages

    c. financial aid is only available for top athletes

    d. there are many types of financial aid available for different types of students including scholarships, grants, loans, and work programs.

7. An example of *investing in human capital* is when you
   a. buy a stock or a bond
   b. purchase a factory to increase the output of a business
   c. stay in school and continue your education
   d. keep your money in cash instead of in a savings account

8. When comparing median weekly incomes of high school dropouts to college graduates, we find that
   a. those who drop out of high school tend to earn more per week than college graduates
   b. those who graduate from college tend to earn over twice as much per week than high school dropouts
   c. high school dropouts and college graduates earn about the same per week
   d. incomes of high school dropouts are increasing faster than incomes of college graduates

9. An example of an *external benefit* of education is when people with college degrees
   a. earn more money due to their education
   b. get more satisfying jobs due to their education
   c. have fun when they attended college
   d. are less likely to be unemployed, poor, and require public assistance

10. Which of the following type of school offers two-year associate degrees at a low cost and often has transfer agreements with four-year colleges?

    a. community colleges

    b. state universities

    c. high schools

    d. Ph.D. programs

11. The Federal Trade Commission (FTC) suggests that you exercise caution before signing a contract or paying any money to attend a

    a. public state university

    b. community college

    c. private vocational school

    d. public high school

12. Where can you find good information about required education and training, earnings, expected job prospects, nature of work and work conditions for hundreds of jobs?

    a. in the *New York Times Week in Review* section

    b. in the *Occupational Outlook Handbook* from the Bureau of Labor Statistics

    c. in your local phone book

    d. in *Us Weekly* magazine

13. Say that you would like to have a job in the foreign travel industry. If nothing else changes, what will happen to your job prospects if more people want to travel to foreign countries over time?

    a. it will likely become harder for you to find a job in the foreign travel industry

    b. it will likely become easier for you to find a job in the foreign travel industry

c. this will likely not change the availability of jobs in the foreign travel industry

d. this will cause fewer people to want to work in the foreign travel industry

14. If your gross pay is $4,000 per month, you can expect that the amount of your monthly paycheck, your net pay, will be

a. more than $4,000 because taxes will be added to your gross pay

b. exactly $4,000

c. $4,000 plus a small bonus if your paycheck is automatically deposited in your bank account

d. less than $4,000 because deductions will be subtracted from your gross pay

15. When a labor union negotiates with an employer for all the workers who are associated with the union, this is called

a. collective bargaining

b. whistle-blower protection

c. the private sector

d. sexual harassment

Compare your work with the answer key found at the end of the Glossary section.

 # Glossary

401(k)   A type of retirement plan offered through some places of employment to help you to save for retirement. With a 401(k), you decide how much you want to contribute toward your retirement and your employer puts the money into an account for you. Your employer's plan would have a selection of investments from which you could choose. Sometimes employers also contribute money to your plan when you decide to contribute.

campus-based aid programs   Three federal student aid programs that are administered directly by the financial aid offices of participating schools. These are the Federal Supplemental Educational Opportunity Grants (FSEOG), Federal Work-Study (FWS), and Federal Perkins Loan programs.

capital   As an economic resource, capital refers to man-made goods that are used to produce other goods and services such as factories, machinery, tools, and equipment.

closed shop   A place of work where only union members can be hired. Closed shops are illegal in states that have right-to-work laws.

collective bargaining   Occurs when a union negotiates with an employer for all the workers who are associated with the union. Union members believe that their chances of receiving better pay and working conditions are greater through collective bargaining than if each worker negotiated with the employer by himself or herself.

college education Postsecondary education obtained at a two-year or four-year college or university, or at a vocational institution. A college education can take different forms depending on the type of school you choose.

community colleges Sometimes called junior colleges, these schools offer two-year programs leading to associate degrees. Students with an associate degree may transfer to a four-year college or university. Community colleges also offer programs leading to certification for specific careers and in this way, their programs may compete with vocational schools.

compulsory education Education that is required by law. In the United States, laws mandating how much education is compulsory are set by individual states.

decentralized education A system of education where most decisions are made at the local level rather than at the national level. The United States has a very decentralized education system.

deductions On your paycheck, the amount subtracted from your gross pay to give you your net pay.

Direct PLUS Loans for Parents Loans that a parent can apply for to pay for a dependent child's education. The parent must have good credit and is responsible for paying off the loan.

disposable income The income that is available to you for spending or saving, after taxes have been paid.

elementary education Also called primary education, elementary education usually includes grades one through six and serves students aged six through 11.

external benefits Benefits of an activity that go to someone other than the consumer or producer. For example, external benefits of education are the benefits that help others in society in addition to you and the provider of your education.

FAFSA The form you use to apply for all types of federal student financial aid. FAFSA stands for Free Application for Federal Student Aid. The form is available at www.fafsa.ed.gov.

federal Pell grant   A need-based grant from the federal government that does not have to be repaid. The amount awarded depends on the student's need, the costs of attending school, and part-time or full-time student status.

fellowships   Like grants, these are financial aid offered by a university or other organization, usually for graduate study.

FICA   A payroll tax, sometimes called an employment tax, used to provide funds for both the Social Security program and the Medicare program. FICA stands for the Federal Insurance Contributions Act.

for-profit schools and colleges   Private institutions that distribute profits earned to owners or shareholders.

four-year college and university   In the United States, higher education institutions that offer a variety of majors and regularly require students to complete a wide variety of courses to receive a broad, general education. In most cases, when someone is a college graduate or receives a college degree, this means that he or she has received a bachelor's degree from a four-year college or university. Although the terms college and university are often used interchangeably, colleges often limit their offerings to four-year undergraduate degrees whereas universities also offer more advanced degrees. Universities are usually larger than colleges and may be organized to contain different colleges such as a college of business and a college of arts and sciences.

grants   With respect to financial aid, grants are most often offered by the federal or state governments. Grants are usually need-based and are usually not tied to special talents or achievements.

gross pay   The total amount you earn in a pay period before any deductions such as taxes are taken out of your paycheck.

high schools   Also called senior high schools, these schools frequently include grades nine or 10 through 12 and serve students aged 14 through 18 in the United States.

human capital   A person's knowledge and skills.

interest   The cost you pay for borrowing money.

interest rate   The percentage of the total amount borrowed that you must pay back in interest.

internship   A type of work experience where you have supervised practical training for a certain job.

investing in human capital   Devoting time and resources to improving your knowledge and skills through education and training.

K-12 education   Education from kindergarten through high school (12th grade) in the United States.

labor force   Those who are 16 years of age or older and not in institutions who are working or looking for work.

labor union   An organization of employees formed to bargain with the employer, usually for better pay, benefits, and working conditions.

major   An area of specialization in a two-year or four-year college or university.

marginal costs   The additional cost of producing or consuming one more unit of something. Marginal costs are sometimes called incremental costs. The marginal costs of going to college are the additional costs you incur to go to college versus doing something else.

master's degree   A type of postsecondary education usually involving two years of advanced study in a specific field such as business or education. A common master's degree is an MBA, or Masters of Business Administration.

median   Half of the series fall above this number and half fall below. For example, median earnings means that half of the people in the category earned above that level of income, and half of the people in that category earned below that level of income.

Medicare   A federal government program that provides hospital insurance benefits for people aged 65 or older. Like Social Security, Medicare is supported by FICA taxes.

merit-based financial aid   Non–need-based financial aid, awarded to students on the basis of achievement, ability, talent, or special characteristics.

middle schools   Also called junior high schools, middle schools deliver the level of education between elementary schools and high schools. There are several different structures for this level of education in the United States.

minor   An area of specialization in college, but with less required course work than for a major.

need-based financial aid   Aid given to students who do not have enough money to pay for their own college education.

net pay   The amount of pay you receive after deductions are taken out.

network   The group of people with whom you are connected.

nonprofit schools and colleges   Private institutions that use any profits earned to achieve the goals of the school rather than distributing profits to owners or shareholders.

on-the-job training   The training and skills a worker learns while at work.

opportunity cost   What you give up when you have to make a choice.

pay stub   The attachment to your paycheck that shows the deductions that were made from your paycheck.

Ph.D.   Also called a doctorate degree, a Ph.D. involves three to five years of graduate study and writing a dissertation involving original research in the chosen field. Ph.D. stands for doctor of philosophy, although Ph.D.'s are earned in many fields and not just in philosophy.

postdoctoral study   Study undertaken soon after completing a Ph.D. involving research to further focus on the area of study. These programs are often funded by a university or other research institution.

postgraduate education   Education received after graduating from a four-year college or university, including work toward master's degrees, doctorate degrees, professional degrees, and postdoctoral study.

postsecondary education   Also called higher education, this refers to education obtained after high school. This is often referred to in general terms as a college education.

private schools and colleges   Those that are not formally affiliated with a government organization.

private sector   The part of the economy that is not controlled by the government.

productivity   Output per hour of work.

professional school   Schools that prepare you for certain professions such as medicine, dentistry, or law. Professional schools are usually part of universities.

promotion   With respect to your job, this means that you are assigned to a higher-level position with more responsibilities.

public schools and colleges   Those that are financed and operated by state and local governments.

raise   With respect to pay, this means that you earn a higher salary and are paid more money for doing your job. Often, getting a raise is associated with getting a promotion.

recession   Occurs when overall output declines in the economy for a sustained period.

regressive tax   A tax where people with lower incomes pay a higher percentage of their income in taxes.

résumé   A short document that provides an easy-to-view summary of information about you.

right-to-work laws   Laws that prohibit requiring workers to join a union in order to keep their jobs.

scholarship   A type of financial aid to further education that does not have to be repaid. Scholarships are often merit-based and awarded on the basis of academic or athletic talent, interest in studying certain subjects, or being part of a certain minority group.

Social Security   A federal government program introduced in the 1930s to provide benefits for retired people, disabled people, and children of deceased workers. Most wage-earners pay FICA taxes, which pay for social security.

Stafford Loans   Low-interest loans for students with financial need to help finance education at a four-year college, community college, or trade school. Students receiving Stafford loans borrow from the U.S. Department of Education through their school.

student loans   Money that you borrow for college and that you must pay back. You usually do not need to begin paying back a student loan until after you have graduated from college.

technology   Factors that increase the output of goods and services from the amount of workers and capital available. Examples of technology are the printing press, the telephone, computers, and the Internet.

undergraduate education   College education obtained before earning a degree from a four-year college or university.

union shop   A place of work where workers are required to join a union. Union shops are prohibited in states that have right-to-work laws.

vocation   The specific career for which you are trained.

vocational or technical schools or colleges   Sometimes also called career or trade schools, these institutions are designed to teach you a specific job or trade.

W-4   A federal form that the Internal Revenue Service (IRS) requires. How you fill in the information at the top of the W-4 form affects how much is withheld from your paycheck.

whistle-blower   Someone who reports that something is wrong in the workplace and hopes that reporting the wrongdoing will help to stop it.

withholding tax   The money that is deducted from your paycheck in advance of the taxes being due.

work-study programs   Program offered by a college where they give you a job or help you find a job so you can earn money to help you pay for your educational expenses. Participating in work-study programs is frequently need-based.

Answer key:

1. C
2. D
3. A
4. B
5. A
6. D
7. C
8. B
9. D
10. A
11. C
12. B
13. B
14. D
15. A

 Bibliography

Baum, Sandy, and Kathleen Payea. "The Benefits of Higher Education for Individuals and Society." College Board. Available online. URL: http://www. collegeboard.com/prod_downloads/press/cost04/ EducationPays2004.pdf. Accessed October 2010.

Bureau of Labor Statistics. "College Enrollment and Work Activity of 2009 High School Graduates." Available online. URL: http://www.bls.gov/news. release/hsgec.nr0.htm. Accessed October 2010.

College Board. "College Search: Find the Right Colleges for You." Available online. URL: http://collegesearch. collegeboard.com/search/index.jsp. Accessed October 2010.

———. "What It Costs to Go to College." Available online. URL: http://www.collegeboard.com/student/ pay/add-it-up/4494.html. Accessed October 2010.

College.gov. "Why Go? What to Do? How to Pay?" Available online. URL: http://www.college.gov/wps/ portal. Accessed October 2010.

Day, Jennifer Cheeseman, and Eric C. Newburger. "The Big Payoff: Educational Attainment and Synthetic Estimates of Work-Life Earnings." Available online. URL: http://www.census.gov/prod/2002pubs/p23-210. pdf. Accessed October 2010.

Federal Trade Commission. "Choosing a Career or Vocational School," Available online. URL: http://www.ftc.gov/bcp/edu/pubs/consumer/products/pro13.shtm. Accessed October 2010.

Hanson, Maria. "9 Tips for Getting a Promotion." Available online. URL: http://www.livecareer.com/news/Career/9-Tips-for-Getting-a-Promotion_$$01381.aspx. Accessed October 2010.

National Association of Financial Aid Administrators. "About Financial Aid." Available online. URL: http://www.nasfaa.org/Advocacy/Students/Apply/About_Financial_Aid.aspx. Accessed October 2010.

Needelman, Sarah E. "Big Blunders Job Hunters Make," Available online. URL: http://online.wsj.com/article/SB10001424052748703615104575328641186507512.htm. Accessed October 2010.

Nemko, Marty. "How to Avoid Getting Fired." Available online. URL: http://www.kiplinger.com/magazine/archives/2006/07/nemko.html?si=1. Accessed October 2010.

U.S. Department of Education. "Student Aid on the Web." Available online. URL: http://studentaid.ed.gov/PORTALSWebApp/students/english/index.jsp. Accessed October 2010.

U.S. Department of Education, National Center for Education Statistics. "Enrollment in Postsecondary Institutions, Fall 2009; Graduation Rates, 2003 & 2006 Cohorts; and Financial Statistics, Fiscal Year 2009," Available online. URL: http://nces.ed.gov/pubs2011/20111230.pdf. Accessed October 2010.

U.S. Department of Education. "10 Facts about K-12 Education Funding." Available online. http://www2.

ed.gov/about/overview/fed/10facts/index.html. Accessed October 2010.

U.S. Department of Labor. "Education Pays." U.S. Bureau of Labor Statistics. Available online. URL: http://www.bls.gov/emp/ep_chart_001.html. Accessed October 2010.

U.S. Department of Labor. *Occupational Outlook Handbook, 2010-2011 Edition.* Bureau of Labor Statistics. Available online. http://www.bls.gov/oco/. Accessed October 2010.

U.S. Department of Labor. O*NET Resource Center. Available online. URL: http://www.onetcenter.org/. Accessed October 2010.

U.S. Department of Labor. "Compliance Assistance." Available online. URL: http://www.dol.gov/compliance/. Accessed October 2010.

Index

Note: *Italic* page numbers refer to tables, charts, and illustrations.

four-year colleges and universities
3, 6–7, 135. *See also* bachelor's
degree (B.A./B.S.)
applying to 70, 73–75
considerations in choosing 62–65,
63, 64–65, 66, 68–72, 69
public v. private 21–22, 71, 72
Free Application for Federal Student
Aid (FAFSA) 32, 134
FWS (Federal Work-Study) 32–33

G

gender, income and 44–45
GLBT-based scholarships 30
government 9–15, 29, 31–34, 53, 54,
97, 108–112. *See also* laws and
legislation
graduate education 78–79. *See also*
doctoral degree (Ph.D.); master's
degree
grants 26–27, 32–33, 135
gross pay 108, 113, 135

H

health and safety laws 123–125
health insurance 110, 112, 113, 122,
123
high school dropouts 40, 41, 42, 43,
53
high school education 2–4, 3, 95, 135
compulsory education 11–12, 54,
134
income and 39–41, 40, 42–43
public v. private 9–11
role of government in 13–15, 14
higher education. *See* college education; postdoctoral study; postgraduate education
human capital 37–38, 44, 136

I

income 107–114, 139
choice of major and 46, 77, 78
effects of educational level on
39–47, 40, 43, 47, 63

effects of race and gender on 44–47
productivity and 43–44, 55, 138
understanding your paycheck
108–113
incremental costs 20–21, 136
insurance plans 110, 112, 113, 122,
123
interest (financial) 27, 136
interests (personal), assessment of
81–85
Internet, as source for finding jobs
96–97
internships 98, 136
interviewing, employment 96,
102–105
investing in human capital 37–38,
44, 136
Iraq and Afghanistan Service Grant
32

J

jobs. *See* employment
junior colleges. *See* community colleges
junior high (middle) school 2, 3, 137

K

K-12 education 2–4, 3, 9–11, 136. *See
also* high school education
compulsory education 11–12, 54,
134
income and 39–41, 40
role of government in 13–15, 14

L

labor force 87–95, 136
labor unions 97, 125–126, 136, 139
laws and legislation 12–15, 23
compulsory education 11–12, 54,
134
licensing of vocational schools
66–67
workplace rules and laws 121–126
leave and sick time 122
letters of recommendation 74–75